HIGH FIDELITY

John Cusack most recently starred in Tim Robbins' *Cradle Will Rock*, and in the dark comedy *Being John Malkovich*, directed by Spike Jonze.

Cusack's other films include Stephen Frears' *The Grifters*, *Eight Men Out*, *Say Anything*, *The Sure Thing*, *Con Air*, *City Hall*, *Bullets Over Broadway*, *Shadows and Fog*, *Midnight in the Garden of Good and Evil* and *Grosse Point Blank*, a film which he also produced and co-wrote under the aegis of his New Crime Productions.

In addition to his film work, Cusack founded New Crime Theatre Company, one of Chicago's foremost avant-garde theatre companies, where he has directed four plays.

D.V. DeVincentis & Steve Pink marked their feature film writing debut with the black comedy *Grosse Point Blank*, which they co-wrote with John Cusack and Tom Jankiewicz. DeVincentis and Pink founded New Crime Theatre in Chicago with John Cusack in 1988, a company they describe as 'a commedia del arte troupe that specializes in absurdist and expressionist theatre.'

Steve Pink also co-produced *Grosse Point Blank* with Cusack and is a partner in their Los Angeles-based New Crime Productions. D.V. DeVincentis is also an associate in New Crime Productions.

Scott Rosenberg's first feature film was the independent movie *Things To Do in Denver When You're Dead*, which he also associate produced. His second feature, *Beautiful Girls*, was directed by Ted Demme and starred Uma Thurman and Matt Dillon. He subsequently wrote the screenplay for Jerry Bruckheimer's *Con Air*, as well as *Disturbing Behaviour*. His forthcoming films include Bruckheimer's *Gone in Sixty Seconds* and New Line Cinema's *A Leonard Cohen Afterworld*. Rosenberg is currently writing the pilot for the Warner Bros. series *Going to California*.

John Cusack

D.V. DeVincentis

Steve Pink

and Scott Rosenberg

HIGH
FIDELITY

based on the novel by

Nick Hornby

FILM FOUR 4

First published 2000 by FilmFour Books
an imprint of Macmillan Publishers Ltd
25 Eccleston Place, London SW1W 9NF
Basingstoke and Oxford

www.macmillan.com

Associated companies throughout the world

ISBN 0 7522 1919 7

9 8 7 6 5 4 3 2 1

A CIP catalogue record for this book is available from
the British Library.

Typeset by Anita Ruddell
Printed and bound in Great Britain by Mackays of Chatham plc,
Chatham, Kent

CAST

Rob   John Cusack

Laura   Iben Hjejle

Dick   Todd Louiso

Barry   Jack Black

Marie De Salle   Lisa Bonet

Charlie   Catherine Zeta-Jones

Liz   Joan Cusack

Ian   Tim Robbins

Vince   Chris Rehmann

Justin   Ben Carr

Sarah   Lili Taylor

Penny   Joelle Carter

Caroline   Natasha Gregson Wagner

Alison Jr. High   Shannon Stillo

Rob Jr. High   Drake Bell

Laura's Mom   Laura Whyte

Anaugh   Sara Gilbert

Barry's Customer   Rich Talarico

Beta Band Customer   Matt O'Neill

Middle Aged Customer   Brian Powell

Rob's Mom   Margaret Travolta

Laura's Sister Jo   Jill Peterson

Minister   Dick Cusack

Girl – 19 year old   Susan Yoo

Paul   Chris Bauer

Miranda   K.K. Dodds

Alison's Mom   Marilyn Dodds Frank

Kevin Bannister   Duke Doyle

Boy in Park   Aaron Himelstein

Chris Thompson   Jonathan Herrington

Rock Guy   Daniel Lee Smith

Mourners   Leah Gale

David Darlow

Marco   Erik Gundersen

Bruce Springsteen   Himself

Louis   Alex Desert

Man in Store   Alan S. Johnson

Party Guests   Ian Belknap

                             Andrew Micheli

                             Polly Noonan

                             Philip Rayburn Smith

                             Michele Graff

                             Susie Cusack

Piano Player   Liam Hayes

Greenday Girl   Damian Rogers

Skateboarder   Robert A. Villanueva

Flea Market Musician   Joe Spaulding

Bartender   Scott A. Martin

Laura's Friend   Heather Norris

CREW

Directed by   Stephen Frears

Written by   D.V. DeVincentis

      & Steve Pink

      & John Cusack

      and Scott Rosenberg

Based upon the book by   Nick Hornby

Produced by   Tim Bevan

      Rudd Simmons

Executive Producers   Mike Newell

      Alan Greenspan

      Liza Chasin

Co-Producers   John Cusack

      D.V. DeVincentis

      Steve Pink

Director of Photography   Seamus McGarvey, B.S.C.

Production Designers   David Chapman

Therese Deprez

Film Editor   Mick Audsley

Costume Designer   Laura Cunningham Bauer

Original Music Composed by   Howard Shore

Music Supervisor   Kathy Nelson

Casting by   Victoria Thomas

HIGH
FIDELITY

**Screenplay by
John Cusack,
D.V. DeVincentis
Steve Pink and
Scott Rosenberg**

FADE IN:

INT. ROB'S APARTMENT. NIGHT.

> *The stereo – not a mini-system, not a matching set, but coveted audiophile clutter of McIntosh and Nakamichi, each component from a different era... The records – big thin LPs. Fields of them. We move across them, slowly... they seem to come to rest in an end of a few books... but then the CDs start, and go on, faster and faster, then the singles, then the tapes... It seems they will never end until... we come to ROB, boyishly handsome and early thirties. He sits in an over-sized beanbag chair, his face unreadable, his head gripped by a big pair of Boudokan head-phones.*

ROB VO   What came first? The music or the misery? People worry about kids playing with guns and watching violent videos. Nobody worries about kids listening to thousands – literally thousands – of songs about broken hearts and rejection and pain and misery and loss. Did I listen to pop music because I was miserable, or was I miser-able because I listened to pop music?

> *We hear what he is hearing, something forebod-ing and upbeat at the same time. He stares at a group of bags huddled next to the door.*

LAURA, ROB's girlfriend, enters the room, and he immediately pulls the headphones off. She clocks him for a moment, catching him in what seems to be an old and repeated moment of non-presence. She begins to pick up the bags. She begins to cry a bit.

LAURA   I don't really know what I'm doing.

ROB   You don't have to go this second. You can stay until whenever.

LAURA   We've done the hard part now. I might as well, you know...

ROB   Well, stay for tonight.

LAURA lifts the last small bag and backs out the door.

INT. APARTMENT STAIRWELL.

LAURA drags her bags, banging down the stairs.

ROB VO   My desert island, all time, top five most memorable break-ups, in chronological order, are as follows: Alison Ashmore, Penny Hardwick, Jackie Alden, Charlie Nicholson, Sarah Kendrew.

INT. ROB'S APARTMENT. NIGHT.

*ROB stares at the shut door for a long moment.
He moves through the living room to an open
window facing the street.*

ROB VO   Those were the ones that really hurt. Can you see
your name in that list, Laura? Maybe you'd sneak
into the top ten, but there's no place for you in
the top five. Sorry. Those places are reserved for
the kind of humiliations and heartbreaks that
you're just not capable of delivering.

*ROB's left hand cranks the volume knob on the
stereo while his right switches the CD changer to
something loud and adrenal. He goes to the window and opens it.*

EXT. ROB'S APARTMENT. NIGHT.

*We see her as a distant figure down the street.
He shouts out of the window.*

ROB   If you really wanted to mess me up, Laura, you
should have got to me earlier.

INT. ROB'S APARTMENT. NIGHT.

*He shuts the window, sits down in his chair, and
lights a defiant cigarette. He looks directly into
camera.*

ROB   Which brings us to number one on the Top Five
All-time Break-up list – Alison Ashmore...

CUT TO

EXT. SUBURBAN PARK. AFTERNOON. 1980.

*A group of junior-high girls across the park, lazily
dangling from swings and talking to each other.
One is putting on make-up.*

ROB VO   One moment they weren't there, not in any form
that interested us anyway, then the next you
couldn't miss them, they were everywhere... and
they had grown breasts... and we wanted... actually, we didn't know what we wanted next, but it
was something interesting, disturbing even...

*One of the girls, ALISON, looks back at us,
breaks from the pack, and heads our way... As
she reaches us we turn to see her loop an arm
through a very nervous YOUNG ROB's arm, and
lead him away from his crew of young boys.*

EXT. SUBURBAN PARK. DUSK. 1980.

*ROB and ALISON sit on the bench, kissing awk-
wardly.*

EXT. PARK BENCH. DUSK.

The same shot, the next night: new clothes, same clumsy make-out session.

ROB VO   My relationship with Alison Ashmore lasted six hours.

EXT. PARK BENCH. DUSK.

The next night...

ROB VO   The two hours after school and before *The Rockford Files*, for three days in a row. On the fourth afternoon...

EXT. SAME PARK BENCH.

...And the fourth night...

ROB VO   Kevin Bannister.

ALISON and another boy, KEVIN BANNISTER. Kissing.

EXT. SUBURBAN PARK. AFTERNOON. 1980.

YOUNG ROB has come over to another BOY. They watch ALISON and KEVIN.

BOY   Slut.

INT. ROB'S APARTMENT. NIGHT.

ROB   It would be nice to think that, since I was fourteen, times have changed, relationships have
become more sophisticated, females less cruel,
skins thicker, but there still seems to be an ele-
ment of that afternoon in everything that has happened to me since.

            CUT TO

INT. ROB'S BATHROOM.

            ROB enters, is confronted by LAURA's plain worn
underwear over radiators.

ROB   Look at these! I used to dream I would be sur-
rounded by exotic underwear for ever and ever.
Now I know women save their best pairs for the
nights they know they're going to sleep with
somebody.

            He throws them in the trash.

EXT. WILSON EL STATION PLATFORM. MORNING.

            ROB sits on a bench at the end of the platform,
headphones around his neck.

ROB   Number two. Penny Hardwick. Penny was great-
looking, and her top five recording artists were

Carly Simon, Carole King, James Taylor, Cat
Stevens and Elton John... Everybody liked Penny.

*He dons headphones and hits play on his
Walkman. 'Crocodile Rock' by Elton John begins
to leak out as we see...*

EXT. LANE TECH. FLASHBACK.

*PENNY, 16, is walking across the grass toward
us. She's the clean, sporty, nice, wholesome girl-
next-door. She waves to off-camera friends, smiling a winning smile.*

ROB VO   She was nice. Nice manners. Nice grades. Nice-
looking. She was so nice, in fact, that she would-
n't let me put my hand underneath, or even on
top of, her bra.

INT. TEENAGE MAKE-OUT PARTY. NIGHT.

*ROB and PENNY mash face. After a beat, ROB's
hand levitates, and moves in on PENNY's breast...*

ROB VO   Attack and defence, invasion and repulsion: it
was as if breasts were little pieces of property
that had been unlawfully annexed by the oppos-
ite sex – they were rightfully ours and we wanted
them back.

...She pushes it gently away.

8

INT. PENNY'S BEDROOM. NIGHT.

> *PENNY and ROB sit on the edge of the bed, kissing. ROB moves his hand up toward the breast, but the hand then seems to have a new idea, and dives south to follow the thigh into PENNY's skirt... when he contacts skin, PENNY rolls away, like a gymnast, off the bed, out of frame. ROB looks away balefully.*

ROB VO   Sometimes I got so bored of trying to touch her breasts that I would try to touch her between her legs – it was like trying to borrow a dollar, getting turned down, and asking for fifty grand instead.

> *CUT TO*

EXT. STREET. NIGHT.

> *ROB walks PENNY to her front door. She is smiling; he seems distant.*

ROB VO   I wasn't interested in Penny's nice qualities, just breasts, and therefore she was no good to me.

> *She leans in to kiss him, and he shrugs her off.*

ROB   What's the point? It never goes anywhere.

> *Without looking at her, ROB turns and walks down the street, getting smaller. PENNY watches for a while.*

ROB VO   She cried, and I hated her for it, because she
          made me feel bad. I started dating a girl who
          everyone said would give it up, and who didn't...

INT. SCHOOL CHEMISTRY LAB. DAY.

          *CHRIS THOMPSON is bragging to ROB, whose
          mouth hangs open.*

ROB VO   And Penny went with this asshole Chris
          Thompson who told me that he had sex with her
          after something like three dates.

          *CLOSE-UP on YOUNG ROB's face, shell-
          shocked.*

          CUT TO

INT. EL TRAIN. MORNING.

          ROB stands with the other commuters.

ROB   Read any women's magazine and you'll see the
          complaint over and over again: men are not inter-
          ested in foreplay. They are selfish, greedy, clum-
          sy, unsophisticated. These complaints, I can't
          help feeling, are kind of ironic, because back
          then, all we wanted was foreplay and girls
          weren't interested. Foreplay changes from some-
          thing boys want to do and girls don't do to
          something that women want and men can't be
          bothered with.

Next to ROB is a woman reading Cosmo.

ROB *(cont'd)* The perfect couple, if you ask me, is the
              Cosmo woman and a fourteen-year-old boy.

              Across from her is sitting a fourteen-year-old boy.

EXT. MILWAUKEE AVENUE. DAY.

              *An old Chicago block of local merchants, on a
              busy street. ROB makes his way down the street,
              jangling a set of keys and talking to us.*

ROB   My store's called Championship Vinyl. It's carefully
              placed to attract the bare minimum of window
              shoppers.

              *ROB arrives at a storefront, and begins unlocking
              a rusty gate with two locks and then a beaten-
              down door.*

ROB *(cont'd)* I get by because of the people who make a
              special effort to shop here – young men, always
              young men, who spend all their time looking for
              deleted Smiths singles and 'original not re-
              released' – underline – Frank Zappa albums.

INT. RECORD STORE. DAY.

> *In near-darkness. More light might penetrate the windows if there weren't so many record-release posters taped to them. A dusty narrow corridor clad in burlap and shag rug. On the walls are bagged 45s.*

ROB   The fetish properties are not unlike porn. I would feel guilty taking their money if I wasn't, kind of, well, one of them.

> *ROB opens the door, and flips a switch, causing the fluorescents to sputter. We see in his eyes the reverence and earnestness of a priest drawn at midnight to his empty church.*

> *The door creaks open behind ROB, admitting DICK, a nervous, forlorn, but sweet and intelligent discophile with long greasy black hair, a Sonic Youth T-shirt, a monstrous pair of headphones, and a canvas record bag emblazoned with a label logo.*

ROB *(cont'd)* Morning, Dick.

DICK   Oh, hi. Hi, Rob.

ROB   Good weekend?

DICK   Yeah, OK. I found the first Licorice Comfits album
            at Vintage Vinyl. The one on Testament of Youth.
            Never released here. Japanese import only.

ROB   Great.

DICK   I'll tape it for you.

ROB   No, that's OK. Really.

DICK   'Cause you said you liked their second one, you
            said, Pop, Girls, etc. The one with Cheryl Ladd
            on the cover. You didn't see the cover though.
            You just had the tape I made you.

ROB   I haven't really absorbed that one yet.

DICK   I'll just make it for you.

            CUT TO

INT. RECORD STORE. LATER.

            *DICK is behind the counter, ROB in the aisles
            with a clipboard doing inventory. Music: Belle and
            Sebastian.*

ROB   *(re: music)* What's this?

DICK   The new Belle and Sebastian. Like it?

The door flies open and BARRY, an acid-tongued post-punk-rock misanthrope without quite enough intelligence to conceptualize his own rebellion, walks in. His teeth are clenched in air-guitar concentration.

BARRY   BAA! BA BA DANG!

DICK shrinks back from him instinctively. He stops mid-step and cocks his ear at the music playing in the store. His face adopts an exaggerated grimace.

BARRY *(cont'd)* Holy shite! What the fuck's this?

DICK   It's the new—

ROB   It's the record we've been listening to and enjoying, Barry.

BARRY moves in on the stereo behind the counter, and DICK gets out of his way.

BARRY   Well, that's problematic because it sucks ass.

He pops the CD out and frisbees it to DICK.

BARRY *(cont'd) (re: the CD)* Yours, I assume...

BARRY pulls a tape out of his jacket and jams it in. 'Walking On Sunshine' by Katrina and the

Waves comes through at the red levels.

ROB *(over the blare)*   TURN IT OFF, BARRY.

BARRY   IT WON'T GO ANY LOUDER.

> *BARRY walks in rhythm toward the stockroom
> and disappears. ROB goes behind the counter
> and stops the tape. BARRY's head pops out of
> the stockroom.*

BARRY   *(cont'd)* All I'm trying to do is cheer us up. Go
          ahead and put on some old, sad-bastard music,
          see if I care.

ROB   I don't want old, sad-bastard music either. I just
          want something I can ignore.

BARRY   But it's my new tape. My Monday-morning tape. I
          made it last night just for today.

ROB   Yeah, well it's fucking Monday afternoon. You
          should get out of bed earlier.

BARRY   Don't you want to hear what's next?

ROB   What's next?

BARRY   Play it.

ROB   Say it.

BARRY   *(sighs)* 'Little Latin Lupe Lu.'

        ROB groans.

DICK   Mitch Ryder and the Detroit Wheels?

BARRY   *(defensive)* No. The Righteous Brothers.

DICK   Oh, well. Never mind.

        BARRY bristles and moves slowly in on DICK.

BARRY   What's wrong with the Righteous Brothers?

DICK   Nothing. I just prefer the other one.

BARRY   Bullshit.

ROB   How can it be bullshit to state a preference?

BARRY   Since when did this shop become a fascist
         regime?

ROB   Since you brought that bullshit tape in.

BARRY   *(sarcastic)* Great. That's the fun of working in a
         record store. Playing crappy pap you don't want
         to listen to. I thought this tape was going to be,
         you know, a conversation stimulator. I was going
         to ask you for your top five records to play on a
         Monday morning and all that, and you just had to
         ruin it.

ROB   *(to camera)* I can't fire them. I hired these guys for
             three days a week but they just started showing
             up every day. That was four years ago.

             *From outside, we hear the sound of skateboard
             wheels clacking and scraping, getting louder.
             ROB, DICK and BARRY stop fighting to listen,
             and take surveillance/defence positions. The door
             swings open to admit VINCE and JUSTIN, two fif-
             teen-year-old skate punks. VINCE's hair is post-
             apocalyptically hacked to different lengths,
             JUSTIN's is uniformly shaven with leopard spots
             dyed in. They enter the store with poker faces
             and do their best browser impersonations. Finally
             JUSTIN plucks a CD and the two move to the
             counter.*

             *VINCE reaches into his deep pocket and pulls out
             a paper cup, with a piece of paper attached that
             says 'PLEASE HELP ME. I'M RETARDED.' He
             pours a mass of change and crumpled singles on
             to the counter.*

ROB *(cont'd)* Hey. Didn't you steal that one already?

INT. RECORD STORE. STOCKROOM. LATER.

> *ROB begins opening boxes of records with a razor as he talks to us.*

ROB   Number three in the top five break-ups was Charlie Nicholson, sophomore year of college.

> *CUT TO*

EXT. COLLEGE QUAD. DAY. FLASHBACK.

> *About twenty feet away we see a tall, thin beauty (CHARLIE). She is speaking animatedly to a friend, driving her points home with a forefinger.*

ROB VO   As soon as I saw her, I realized she was the kind of girl I had wanted to meet ever since I'd been old enough to want to meet girls.

INT. CAFÉ. DAY.

> *A younger ROB sits opposite CHARLIE, who is talking animatedly. She circles a paragraph in the book in front of her and turns it around for him to read. He reads, nodding, then looks up and begins to speak. She watches him, then leans in and kisses him deeply. He's taken aback but goes with it.*

ROB VO   She was different. Dramatic. Exotic. She talked a
          lot and when she talked she said interesting
          things about music, books, film and politics. You
          didn't have those terrible, strained silences that
          seemed to characterize most of my relationships.
          And kissing her was her version of oxygen.

EXT. DAMEN AVENUE. AFTERNOON.

          *ROB and CHARLIE walk arm in arm, ROB in cool
          clothes and sunglasses trying to look cool,
          CHARLIE making a point about something. ROB
          checks out how cool he looks with her as they
          walk by a store window. Reflection.*

ROB VO   We went out for two years, and I never got com-
          fortable. Why would a girl – no, a woman — like
          Charlie go out with me?

INT. STAIRWELL. DAY.

          *ROB follows CHARLIE upstairs, carrying shop-
          ping bags. She unzips her jacket and turns a cor-
          ner out of view.*

ROB VO   I felt like a fraud. I felt like all those people who
          suddenly shaved their heads and said they'd
          always been punks. I was sure I would be dis-
          covered at any second.

> ROB finds her jacket on the landing, her shirt a
> few more stairs up, and finally, above, CHARLIE
> staring down the stairs at him, smiling, in only her
> trousers and bra.

ROB VO *(cont'd)* I worried about my abilities as a lover.

INT. CHARLIE'S APARTMENT. DAY.

> The fabulous sophomore design student's studio
> apartment: white wood floor, white walls, over-
> varnished door, Doisneau print on the wall, futon
> on the floor. ROB lies back on his elbows, watch-
> ing CHARLIE in uncomfortable, worried awe. She
> stands, her back to him, wearing only her under-
> wear and pulling on a T-shirt – a heartbreaking
> image to look back on.

ROB VO   I was intimidated by the other men in her design
department, and became convinced that she was
going to leave me for one of them.

> CHARLIE turns around and looks at ROB with
> naked ambivalence.

ROB VO *(cont'd)* She left me for one of them. Marco.

EXT. CHARLIE'S APARTMENT. NIGHT.

> *It is raining like crazy, and ROB is shouting up at a lit window, maniacally gesturing. The curtains part and CHARLIE's figure appears, clad only in a sheet. Next to her is a tall, built, handsome man, MARCO, also in a sheet. Eventually he falls to his knees with a splash and buries his head in his hands. The light goes out.*

ROB VO   And I lost it. I lost it all. Dignity, faith, fifteen pounds...

EXT. DAMEN AVENUE. NIGHT.

> *ROB wandering through the rain.*

ROB VO   ...any small idea of personal identity that I had acquired up to that point.

INT. SOME RECORD STORE. DAY.

> *A younger and catatonic ROB listlessly sorts through a stack of records.*

ROB VO   I came to three months later, and to my surprise had flunked out of school and started working in a record store.

INT. RECORD STORE. STOCKROOM. PRESENT.

ROB sorts through the stacks, in almost the same physical position as above.

ROB   Some people never get over 'Nam or the night
        their band opened for Nirvana. I guess I never
        really got over that girl. What I learned from the
        Charlie debacle is that you gotta punch your
        weight. Charlie was out of my class: too pretty,
        too smart, too witty, too much. What am I? A
        middleweight. Not the smartest guy in the world,
        but certainly not the dumbest. I've read books
        like *The Unbearable Lightness of Being*, and *Love
        in the Time of Cholera*, and understood them –
        they're about girls, right? – just kidding. But I'd
        have to say my all-time favourite book is Johnny
        Cash's autobiography, *Cash* by Johnny Cash. I
        look through the *New Yorker* when my neigh-
        bour's done with it, and I'm not averse to subtitled
        films, although on the whole I prefer American
        films. Top five being *Blade Runner* – director's
        cut, *Cool Hand Luke*, the first two *Godfathers*
        which we'll count as one, *Taxi Driver*, and *Harold
        and Maude*—

The phone rings and ROB grabs it.

ROB *(cont'd)* Championship.

LAURA   *(out of shot)* Hi.

22

ROB   ...Hi.

INT. LAURA'S OFFICE. INTERCUT.

LAURA's tone changes; ROB goes red.

LAURA   I was thinking I could come by the house and
           pick up some stuff while you're at work tomor-
           row.

ROB   While I'm at work. Why while I'm at work?

LAURA   Oh, boy...

ROB   That's what you have to say? 'Oh, boy'? Bravo.

LAURA   Shit, Rob... I gotta go...

INT. RECORD STORE. STOCKROOM. DAY.

Click. She's hung up.

*ROB hears the bell on the front door ring, and he
stops and listens, looks a bit worried.*

CUSTOMER *(out of shot)* I'm looking for a record for my
         daughter. For her birthday. 'I Just Called To Say I
         Love You.' Do you have it?

BARRY   *(out of shot)* Oh yeah. We got it.

ROB relaxes and goes back to work.

CUSTOMER *(out of shot)* Great. Can I have it then?

BARRY   *(out of shot)* No, you can't.

ROB deflates, shaking his head.

INT. RECORD STORE. STOCK FLOOR.

BARRY leans back, elbows up on the counter behind him, talking to the CUSTOMER, a middle-aged, graying man in a raincoat.

CUSTOMER   Why not?

BARRY   Because it's sentimental tacky crap, that's why not. Go to the mall and stop wasting our time.

CUSTOMER   What's your problem—

BARRY   Do you even know your daughter? There is no way she likes that song. Or is she in a coma?

The CUSTOMER throws up his hands and starts out of the store.

CUSTOMER   Okay, okay, buddy. I didn't know it was Pick on the Middle-Aged Square Guy Day. My apologies. I'll be on my way.

He heads for the door.

BARRY   Oh, listen: there's a big black 'X' on the sidewalk just outside the door with a grand piano suspended above it. Could you just stand out there for a second?

CUSTOMER   FUCK YOU!
                    ROB standing in the doorway of the stockroom. He feigns applause.

ROB   Nice, Barry.

BARRY   Rob. Top five musical crimes perpetrated by Stevie Wonder in the '80s and '90s?

ROB's face begins to redden with anger.

ROB   Barry, I'm fucking broke!

BARRY   He was gonna buy one record – which we didn't even have – and leave and never come back again anyway.

ROB   What did he ever do to you?

BARRY   He offended me with his terrible taste.

ROB   It wasn't even his terrible taste. It was his daughter's.

BARRY   Oh, now you're defending that fucking butt-
          munch? You're going soft in your old age, Rob.
          Now all of a sudden I'm offending your golf
          buddy.

          ROB is red and seething.

BARRY *(cont'd)* And by the way, I tell you this for your own
          good: that's the worst sweater I've ever seen. It's
          a Cosby sweater. I have never seen a sweater
          that bad worn by anyone I'm on speaking terms
          with. Did Laura let you leave the house like that?

          *ROB springs on BARRY, grabbing him by the
          lapels and jerking him up against the wall. ROB is
          so mad he can't say anything.*

DICK   Hey, guys... Hey.

          *ROB runs out of steam and drops BARRY, who
          back-pedals fast.*

BARRY   *(extremely shaken)*   What are you, some kind of
          fucking maniac? If this jacket's torn you're gonna
          pay big.

          *BARRY stomps out of the store. ROB turns and
          goes back to the stockroom. DICK follows him in.*

INT. STOCKROOM.

> *DICK appears in the doorway, terrified.*

DICK   Are you all right?

ROB   Laura and I broke up. She's gone. And if we ever see Barry again maybe you can tell him that.

DICK   'Course I will, Rob. No problem. No problem at all. I'll tell him next time I see him.

> *ROB nods. DICK sets out into the uncharted conversational territory of interpersonal relationships.*

DICK *(cont'd)* I've ah... got some other stuff to tell him anyway. I'll just tell him about Laura, when I tell him the other stuff.

ROB   Fine.

DICK   Rob, look. Do you want to... talk about it, that kind of thing?

> *ROB looks up at DICK, who is so nervous that his brow is wet.*

ROB   No. Thanks though, Dick.

> *DICK sighs with relief, and smiles his way out of the stockroom. ROB rubs his face with his hands and stares at the wall.*

INT. ROB'S APARTMENT. NIGHT.

> *ROB enters and presses play on the answering machine. A pleasant, older female voice is heard. It's JANET, LAURA's mother.*

JANET   *(on machine)* Hello, you two. Laura, it's your mother. Your father's angina is a little rough today and I thought he'd like to talk to you. No big deal. I love you too. Oh, listen—

> *ROB jabs the stop button on the machine. ROB goes to his records and begins pulling LPs off of the shelves. He works in a studied, ritualistic manner.*

ROB   So, Charlie and I didn't match. Marco and Charlie matched. Me and Sarah, number four on the all-time list, matched.

EXT. PROMONTORY POINT. THE PAST.

> *ROB and SARAH, a thin, modestly attractive young woman, walk and talk. They seem to be emphatically complaining together.*

ROB VO   She was sad, in the original sense of the word. She had been dumped by some asshole.

SARAH   Michael. Such an asshole.

ROB VO   He was her moment, Charlie was mine.

ROB   I know exactly what you mean.

ROB VO   Sarah had sworn off men. I had sworn off
women.

SARAH   It's just all so painful. And draining. I'm just going
to take some time and be by myself.

ROB   Me too.

They look at each other, and kiss for the first time.

INT. SARAH'S APARTMENT. NIGHT.

*ROB sits up in bed, staring at the television.
SARAH sleeps next to him.*

ROB VO   We were frightened of being left alone for the rest
of our lives. Only people of a certain disposition
are frightened of being left alone for the rest of
our lives at twenty-six.

*In her sleep, SARAH reaches over and takes
ROB's hand.*

INT. SARAH'S KITCHEN. DAY. ROB'S POINT OF VIEW.

    SARAH is sitting across the table, mid-confes-
    sion.

ROB VO   When she told me that she met someone else—

SARAH   Just... someone else.

ROB VO   – it was contrary to the whole spirit of our
           arrangement.

INT. SARAH'S APARTMENT BUILDING HALLWAY. DAY.

    ROB comes out of SARAH's apartment, in a
    daze, and continues down the hall away from us.
    The door shuts behind him.

ROB VO   All we really had in common was that we were
           dumped by people. We were violently anti-dump.

INT. ROB'S APARTMENT. NIGHT.

    He looks to camera, standing among stacks of
    records piled high on the floor.

ROB   So how come I got dumped?

    The doorbell rings, snapping him out of it. He
    goes to the door and opens it – it's DICK.

DICK   Hi, Rob.

ROB   What is it, Dick?

DICK   We're going to Lounge Ax, Marie De Salle's play-
        ing. I like her, you know, she's kind of Sheryl
        Crowish crossed with a post-Partridge Family,
        pre-*LA Law* Susan Dey... but, you know, good.
        Just thought you might like to come. Barry
        thought so too. Really.

ROB   Thanks, but I'm reorganizing my records tonight.
DICK   *(completely understands)* Ahh. Chronologically?

ROB   Nope.

DICK   Alphabetically?

ROB   Nope. Autobiographically.

DICK   Nice.

ROB   I'll be able to see how I got from Deep Purple to
        Howlin' Wolf in twenty-five moves. If I wanna find
        Landslide by Fleetwood Mac, I have to remember
        that I bought it for someone in the fall of 1983
        and then didn't give it to them for personal reas-
        ons.

DICK   That sounds...

ROB   Comforting.

DICK   Yeah.

ROB   It is.

DICK   Okay. Well, see you tomorrow.

ROB   Bye.

             *ROB shuts the door and the phone rings. He
             picks it up.*

MOM   *(out of shot)* Hi, Rob. It's your mother.

             ROB deflates a bit.

ROB   Hi, Mom.

INT. ROB'S MOM'S HOUSE. NIGHT. INTERCUT.

MOM   Everything all right?

ROB   Great. Super-fantastic.

MOM   How's the store?

             She doesn't wait for a reply.

MOM *(cont'd)* You're lucky Laura's doing so well. If it wasn't
             for her, I don't think either of us would ever sleep.

ROB   She left. She's gone.

MOM   What do you mean? Where did she go?

ROB   How would I know? Gone. Girlfriend. Leave. Not say where gone. Laura move out.

MOM   Well, call her mother.

ROB   She just called. She doesn't even know. It's probably the last time I'll ever hear her voice. You spend Christmas at somebody's house, and you see them in their bathrobe, and... I dunno...

           Silence.

ROB *(cont'd)* There'll be another mom and another Christmas. Right?

           The sound of soft crying.

ROB *(cont'd)* I'm all right, if that's what's upsetting you.

MOM   You know that's not what's upsetting me.

ROB   Well, it fucking should be, shouldn't it?

MOM   I knew this was going to happen. What are you going to do, Rob?

ROB   I'm going to drink this bottle of wine, watch TV

and go to bed. Then tomorrow I'll get up and go to work.

MOM   And after that?

ROB   Meet a nice girl and have children. I promise the next time we talk I'll have it all figured out.

MOM   I knew this was going to happen.

ROB   Then what are you getting so upset about?

MOM   Do you know why she left?

ROB   It's got nothing to do with marriage.

MOM   So you say.

ROB   Mom! I'm telling you, Laura didn't want to get married! She is not that kind of girl. That's not what happens now.

MOM   Well I don't know what happens now, apart from you meet someone, you move in, she goes. You meet someone, you move in, she goes.

Silence. ROB busted.

ROB   Shut up, Mom.

INT. EL TRAIN. NIGHT.

> *ROB on the train.*

ROB VO   I liked her right away.

EXT. CLUB. NIGHT. YEARS AGO.

> *ROB and LAURA at the door of the club. They seem to flirt, a few of her friends are on the street a few yards behind her, giggling.*

EXT. LOUNGE AX CLUB, LINCOLN AVENUE. NIGHT.

ROB VO   It was just good. But really good.

> *ROB's face falls. He jerks off his headphones as he arrives at the short line to enter the club. He points to an alley across the street.*

ROB   John Dillinger was shot dead in that alley in a hail of FBI gunfire. You know who tipped them off? His fucking girlfriend. He just wanted to go to the movies, and she—

> *From inside he hears a guitar, playing a tune that becomes familiar not only to ROB, but to us. When a strong, lilting female voice begins to sing, we hear what it is: 'Baby I Love Your Way' by Peter Frampton.*

ROB *(cont'd) (to a DOORMAN)* Is that Peter fucking
Frampton?

The DOORMAN nods.

INT. LOUNGE AX CLUB. NIGHT.

*As ROB enters he looks to the stage, where
MARIE DE SALLE is standing alone with her
acoustic guitar, singing the unfortunate song.
ROB smiles at first, but begins to darken as
the verse continues. Is he beginning to cry?
Yes, he is... MARIE is beautiful, and MARIE has
touched his heart. He tries to fight his feelings,
but gives up.*

ROB   I find myself in two contradictory states.
Suddenly for the first time, I miss Laura with a
passion. I also fall in love with Marie De Salle. In
the exact same second.

*His expression begins to shift from the melan-
choly to something else altogether.*

ROB   *(cont'd)* These things happen. They happen to
me, anyway. This is why I shouldn't be listening
to pop music at the moment.

*ROB navigates toward her through the small
crowd. As he gets closer to the stage—*

DICK   ROB!

          ROB looks over to see DICK sitting with BARRY,
          a few feet away. He shakes it off and sits with
          them, extending a meaningful hand to BARRY,
          who takes it. They turn back to the stage as
          MARIE finishes the song.

ROB   I always hated this song.

DICK AND BARRY   Yeah.

ROB   But now I kind of like it.

          DICK and BARRY nod, then keep watching. All
          three of them are in their own private fantasies
          with MARIE.

DICK   She should've done it on *The Number Four With*
          a Smile.

BARRY   Wasn't her album called *Number Four With a*
          Smile?

DICK   That's what I said.

BARRY   No, no, no, you said *The Number Four With a*
          Smile, and there's no 'The' at the front of the title
          of the album.

DICK   It's a reference to a Chinese meal in Toronto and
            I think that there is a 'The'. But I could be
            wrong.

BARRY   You can be and are wrong.

            *They drop it, so that their eyes can drift back to
            MARIE.*

BARRY   *(cont'd)* I wanna date a musician...

ROB   *(nods in agreement)* I wanna live with a musician.
            She'd write songs at home, ask me what I
            thought of them, maybe even include one of our
            private jokes in the liner notes.

BARRY   ...Maybe a picture of me in the liner notes...

DICK   Just in the background somewhere.

            *MARIE's song ends and she smiles out over the
            room. The audience applauds.*

MARIE   Thank you, guys. I know I'm not supposed to like
            that song, but I do. If anybody wants to buy one
            of my tapes they're five bucks up here. One of
            my other personalities will be selling them.

            CUT TO

FOOT OF THE STAGE.

> *DICK and BARRY wait nervously to buy a tape,*
> *ROB just behind them. MARIE processes sales*
> *with polite monosyllables, until the three get up*
> *front. ROB hands her a ten and she roots around*
> *in a duffel bag for change.*

DICK   So... you live in Chicago now?

MARIE   Yup. Not far from here, actually.

ROB   You like it?

MARIE   It's okay. Hey. You guys might be the sort to know. Are there any good record stores around here, or do I have to go downtown?

> *BARRY and DICK do not try to control them-*
> *selves. They point to ROB.*

DICK   He's got one! On Clark Street!

BARRY   Championship Vinyl. We work there!

DICK   You'd love it!

> *MARIE laughs.*

MARIE   What do you sell?

BARRY   A little of anything that matters.

ROB   Rock, soul, R&B, punk rock, hip-hop, trip-hop,
          ska, new wave, electronica...

MARIE   Sounds great.

          *The line behind them is moving in, and MARIE
          smiles at them and turns to someone else. They
          scurry back toward their table.*

ROB   What did you tell her about the shop for?

BARRY   I didn't know it was classified information. I
          mean, I know we don't have any customers, but I
          thought that was a bad thing, not, like, a busi-
          ness strategy.

          *ROB looks over BARRY at MARIE. She catches
          his eye as she looks over the room. His eyes
          shoot to the floor.*

INT. ROB'S APARTMENT. NIGHT.

          *ROB shuts the door behind him, seemingly
          relieved to be at home. His usual first stop is the
          stereo, where he puts on MARIE's tape. Over to
          the answering machine: Flashing '1.' He hits Play.*

MACHINE   Rob, it's Liz. Just calling to see, well, if you're
           okay. Give me a ring. I'm not taking sides. Yet.
           Lots of love. Bye.

           Beep. He walks out of the room.

INT. ROB'S APARTMENT. MORNING.

           *ROB sits in his chair, still in his pyjamas. He is
           watching the knob on the door turn. The door
           opens and LAURA enters. She sees him and
           stops in her tracks.*

LAURA   Jesus. What are you doing here?

ROB   Took the morning off.
LAURA   C'mon, Rob...

ROB   Do you still love me?

LAURA   Well, it's not really the issue, is it?

ROB   What do you mean? What else is there?

LAURA   I don't know. But bringing it up doesn't solve
           anything. It doesn't change the way we don't get
           along. At all. In fact, I hope we're not in love any-
           more, to be honest. It would give me a better
           opinion of love right now...

ROB   C'mon, Laura. What is this? Did I beat you? Did I
         tell you you were a bad person? What the fuck?
         What should I have done to make you happy?

LAURA   Nothing. Make yourself happy. You can start
         there.

ROB   I'm happy.

LAURA   No, you're not.

ROB   I'm not happy. Why am I not happy?

LAURA   Because you're the same person you used to be.
         And I'm not, and all I've done is changed jobs.

ROB   And hairstyles and clothes and attitude and
         friends and...

LAURA   Look, I couldn't go to work with my hair dyed
         pink. And I can afford to go shopping more now,
         and I've met a couple of people I like over the
         last year or so. Which leaves attitude. That has
         changed.

ROB   You're tougher.

LAURA   More confident maybe.

ROB   Harder.

LAURA   Less neurotic. You haven't changed so much as a
         pair of socks since I've known you. Are you intend-
         ing to stay the same for the rest of your life?

ROB   I'm all right.

LAURA   Yeah, you're all right. But you're not great. And
         you're certainly not happy. So what happens if
         you get happy? And yes, I know, that's the title of
         an Elvis Costello album. I use the reference delib-
         erately to catch your attention.

ROB   You're the one who hates your job.

LAURA   See? You haven't got a clue. I like my job. I'm not
         exactly who I wanted to be when I grew up but—

ROB   Who did you want to be?

         LAURA sits.

LAURA   Not some woman in a suit with a secretary. I
         wanted to be a legal-aid lawyer with a DJ
         boyfriend.

ROB   So quit the firm and find yourself a DJ. What do
         you want me to do about it?

         LAURA sighs and stands.

LAURA   Look. All I'm saying is, you have to allow for
           things to happen to people, most of all to your-
           self. And you don't, Rob. So what's the use?

           ROB says nothing. She leaves.

INT. RECORD STORE. DAY.

           *ROB, DICK and BARRY stand around talking to
           LOUIS, a record collector, who holds a stack of
           LPs in his hands. BARRY is behind the counter.*

LOUIS   Your turn, Rob.

ROB   Okay. I'm feeling basic. Top five side one track
           ones. Number one... 'Janie Jones', The Clash,
           from *The Clash*.

BARRY   Ehh.

ROB   'Thunder Road,' Bruce Springsteen, from *Born to
           Run*. 'Smells Like Teen Spirit,' Nirvana,
           Nevermind.

BARRY   Oh no, Rob, that's not obvious enough. Not at all.
           How about 'Point Of No Return' on *Point Of No
           Return*? Louis, are you listening to this?

ROB   Shut up. 'Let's Get It On,' Marvin Gaye, from
           Let's Get It On.

LOUIS   That would be on my list.

BARRY   Though not on mine.

           LOUIS rolls his eyes.

ROB   'Airbag,' Radiohead, from *OK Computer*.

BARRY   *(sarcastic)* Ooh! Oh God! A kind of recent record!

           *A strange-looking MAN enters the store, and
           comes up to the counter.*

BARRY *(cont'd) (to the MAN)* In a minute— *(to ROB)* Nice,
           Rob. A sly declaration of new classic status
           slipped into a list of old safe ones! Pussy! *(To the
           MAN)* In a minute! *(To ROB)* Couldn't you make it
           any more obvious than that? What about the
           Beatles? What about fucking... fucking
           Beethoven? Track one, side one of the Fifth
           Symphony? How can someone with no interest in
           music own a record store?

           The MAN addresses BARRY nervously.

MAN   Excuse me. Do you still have that Captain
           Beefheart French import? *Safe As Milk*?

           *BARRY scratches his chin, and goes behind the
           counter to a box of rarities. The others watch on,
           sensing what's coming.*

BARRY   Let's see...

He plucks it from the box and hands it to the MAN.

BARRY *(cont'd)* Here.

MAN   Wow. Yeah. Um, how much is it?

BARRY takes it from him, turns it over.

BARRY   Yeah, you know, I don't think I'm selling it this
          week. Maybe next week.

*He sticks it back in the box. ROB and DICK sup-
press a snort of laughter.*

MAN   But... you said that last week.

BARRY   Did I? Yeah, well...

*The MAN turns and stomps out of the store,
humiliated. BARRY smiles at ROB and DICK, who
smile back.*

DICK   Nicely played.

LOUIS   I don't have that record. I'll give you forty for it.

BARRY   Rob?

ROB   Sold.

LOUIS   Why sell it to me and not him?

BARRY   'Cause you're not a geek, Louis.

LOUIS   You guys are snobs.

DICK   No, we're not.

LOUIS   Seriously, you're totally elitist. You feel like the
         great, unappreciated scholars. So you shit on
         people who know less than you—

ROB, DICK AND BARRY   No—

LOUIS   —Which is everybody.

ROB, DICK AND BARRY   Yes.

LOUIS   It's sad, that's all.

BARRY   Well, thanks for the breakdown, Herr Freud. I
         guess you better get out there in the sunshine
         and find your ass a new record store.

         *ROB takes the record from BARRY and
         regards it.*

ROB   No sale. I haven't taped it yet. Why don't you
         come back next week?

         LOUIS sighs and walks out.

INT. RECORD STORE. STOCKROOM. DAY.

> *From the speakers comes a cleaner studio ver-*
> *sion of 'Baby I Love Your Way' by Marie De Salle.*
> *ROB enters, shuts the door tight behind him,*
> *picks up the phone and dials.*

ROB   I'm sick of the sight of this place. Some days I'm
afraid I'll go berserk, throw the Country A through
K rack out on to the street, go off to work in a
Virgin Megastore and never come back—

INT. LIZ'S OFFICE. DAY. INTERCUT.

LIZ   *(out of shot)* Hello.

ROB   Hi, Liz...

LIZ   Hey, Rob.

ROB   Yeah. Listen. I just wanted to thank you for that
message last night. It made me feel like... less of
an asshole.

LIZ   How're you holding up?

ROB   I'm fine. Great. In fact I've been thinking maybe
it's time to move on. Maybe we're just not right
for each other. Or maybe we are. But time will tell
and at this point. You know?

LIZ   Yeah. I don't want to take sides. And I like Laura
with you. You guys are good together. I don't
think much of this Ian guy—

DICK bursts in, huge-faced.

DICK   Rob! Marie De Salle is in the store!

*ROB freezes, he and DICK turn to the speaker,
which cranks MARIE's voice.*

ROB   Hey, Liz, I gotta go...

FRONT ROOM.

*ROB moves up the aisle fast toward the stereo
where he turns MARIE's music off. He takes a
deep breath and looks up, meeting her eyes.*

ROB   Oh. Hi.

MARIE smiles.

MARIE   *(re: music, joking)* Don't you like my music?

ROB   No, no, I love it, it's just, you must be so sick of
it... Excuse me a minute.

*He reaches back and puts it back on. He cracks
his face into a smile, then walks fast back to the
stockroom door. MARIE watches him go.*

STOCKROOM.

> *As soon as he crosses the threshold his fist clenches and he grimaces.*

ROB   WHAT FUCKING IAN GUY?!

> *CUT TO*

EXT./INT. ROB'S BUILDING'S LOBBY. NIGHT.

> *ROB walks quickly down the street, looking like shit.*

ROB   *(to himself)* Laura doesn't know anybody called Ian. There's no Ian at her office. She has no friends named Ian.

> *ROB enters the building and walks to the mail table in the lobby. He sifts through envelopes for his.*

ROB *(cont'd)* She has never met anyone called Ian in her whole life. I am almost certain that she has lived in an Ian-less universe.

> *He slows... and stops. His face gets a little paler as he lifts a letter up to his face.*
>
> *CLOSE-UP: letter. A cable service bill to a Mr I. Raymond. ROB as he looks at it, divining.*

ROB *(cont'd)* 'I. Raymond.' Ray. 'I.' IAN.

> *CUT TO*

INT. APARTMENT BUILDING HALLWAY. NIGHT.

> *ROB stomps up the stairs talking to camera.*

ROB   Mr I. Raymond. 'Ray' to his friends, and more importantly, to his neighbours. The guy who up until about six weeks ago lived upstairs. I start to remember things now: his stupid clothing, his Leo Sayer hair, his music – Latin, Bulgarian, whatever fucking world music was trendy that week – stupid laugh, awful cooking smells.

> *He opens the door to his apartment and enters...*

ROB *(cont'd)* I never liked him much then, and I fucking hate him now...

INT. ROB'S APARTMENT. NIGHT.

> *Darkness. We move silently through the rooms, and enter the bedroom... closer to the bed, we see ROB on his back, sheets held clenched up to his chin. He stares at the ceiling, sadly.*

> *JUMP CUT TO*

*Almost the same shot. ROB and LAURA in the
bed, semi-tangled. LAURA has a book in her lap.
A creaking is heard. They look up at the light fix-
ture, which shakes a little faster, with the rhythm
of the creaking. Someone is definitely having sex
upstairs, and they are going for it.*

ROB   Jeez. He goes on long enough.

LAURA   I should be so lucky.

They turn to each other and laugh.

JUMP CUT BACK TO

ROB lying still in bed, staring at the ceiling.

ROB'S IAN–LAURA SEX NIGHTMARE. QUICK CUTS.

*IAN mercilessly savages LAURA from behind,
below and above, champagne showers, toe-suck-
ing and animal screams.*

ROB VO   You are as abandoned and as noisy as any char-
         acter in a porn film, Laura. You are Ian's play-
         thing, responding to his touch with shrieks of
         orgasmic delight. No woman in the history of the
         world is having better sex than the sex you are
         having with Ian in my head.

*Back to ROB in bed, imploding with disgust and
sorrow. Tears run down his cheeks into his ears.*

ROB VO   Number five – Jackie Alden. My break-up with
         Jackie Alden had no effect on my life whatsoever.
         I just slotted her in to bump you out of position,
         but now, congratulations, Laura. You made it into
         the top five. Number five with a bullet. Welcome.

INT. RECORD STORE. DAY.

*DICK and BARRY are stocking the racks. ROB
stands at the register, rocking back and forth sort
of like an idiot, to 'Always And Forever' by the
Commodores. He is a mess.*

FEMALE VOICE   Hey.

*ROB looks up to see a nineteen- or twenty-year-
old GIRL standing in front of him.*

GIRL   Do you have soul?

*ROB smiles bitterly at her, clearly having a differ-
ent meaning in mind.*

ROB   That all depends.

The phone rings and ROB picks it up.

ROB *(cont'd)* Championship Vinyl... Hold on a sec – *(to the girl)* back row. *(Back to the phone)* Yeah... How many? What's your address?

>*We hear the door slam off camera, and ROB looks up.*

>*LIZ stands in front of him, and she is mad as hell.*

ROB *(cont'd)* Hi, Liz.

LIZ   YOU FUCKING ASSHOLE!

INT. GREEN MILL.

>*ROB sits at the bar and drinks. Behind him is a plaque that reads, 'Al Capone drank here. Often.'*

ROB   For a couple of years I was a DJ at a club...

INT. DOUBLE DOOR. NIGHT. YEARS AGO.

>*ROB in a DJ booth, a big grin on his face. Below him is a full floor rocking to the beat.*

ROB VO   I was good at it, I think, and while I was doing it I was the happiest I've ever been. And that's where I met Laura.

>*ROB is trying to find the next record before the one on the table ends – he's in a rush. A face*

*appears before him that makes him slow down –
LAURA. She's done up in a leather jacket, spiky
hair and mod-ish make-up.*

ROB VO *(cont'd)* She was already a lawyer, but she worked
for legal aid, hence the leather jacket and the
clubbing.

She smiles, points at the turntable.

LAURA   Hey, that's a kick-ass record. Where do I get it?

INT. GREEN MILL. PRESENT.

*A slumped ROB looks at us in the mirror behind
the bar.*

ROB   I liked her right away.

EXT. DOUBLE DOOR. NIGHT. YEARS AGO.

*ROB and LAURA at the door of the club. They
seem to flirt, a few of her friends are on the street
a few yards behind her, giggling.*

ROB   Listen. Come next week and I'll have a tape for
you.

INT. GREEN MILL. PRESENT.

ROB   To be honest, I hadn't met anyone as promising

as Laura since I started DJ-ing, and meeting promising women is partly what the DJ-ing was supposed to be about.

INT. ROB'S APARTMENT. NIGHT. YEARS AGO.

ROB's hands move records and CDs around industriously.

INT. DOUBLE DOOR. NIGHT. YEARS AGO.

ROB stands at the base of the booth, talking closely with LAURA. He hands her the tape.

INT. RAINBO CLUB. NIGHT. YEARS AGO.

ROB and LAURA have beer and laugh uncontrollably. They can't stop and it goes on and on...

ROB VO   And we went on from there. She lost her lease on her apartment in Lakeview, she moved in with me and it stayed that way for years.

INT. MOVIE THEATRE. NIGHT. YEARS AGO.

ROB and LAURA watch a movie.

ROB VO   And she didn't make me miserable, or anxious, or ill at ease. It sounds boring but it wasn't. It wasn't spectacular either.

INT. ROB AND LAURA'S APARTMENT. MORNING. YEARS AGO.

ROB and LAURA make sweet love.

INT. GREEN MILL. PRESENT.

ROB in his reverie.

ROB   It was just... good. Really good.

He almost drifts off.

ROB   *(cont'd)* So how come suddenly I'm an asshole?

INT. SMITH AND WOLLENSKI. LUNCH HOUR.

LAURA enters and greets a woman at a table. When the woman stands we see she is LIZ.

Scene is intercut with ROB addressing camera in Green Mill.

ROB   I get the feeling that since our phone call Liz has talked to Laura and Liz stuck up for me, and Laura filled her in on a few things.

LIZ and LAURA sit across from each other, LIZ is speaking to LAURA, who silently fumes. LAURA silences LIZ with her hand, leans forward and begins speaking quickly and intensely. She seems to be ticking off points with her fingers.

ROB   *(cont'd)* I don't know what, precisely, Laura said, but she would have revealed at least two, maybe even all four, of the following pieces of information: one — that I slept with somebody else—

LAURA   —He slept with somebody else—

ROB   —While she, Laura, was pregnant.

LAURA   —While I was pregnant.

ROB   Two: that my affair contributed directly to her—

LAURA   —Pretty much directly to—

ROB   —Terminating the pregnancy.

LIZ leans back, her face first mortified then blank with anger.

LIZ   NO.

ROB   Three: that after her abortion, I borrowed a large sum—

LAURA   —Four grand or so—

ROB VO   —Of money from her and have not yet repaid any
          of it.

LIZ   Bastard!

ROB VO   Four: that, shortly before she left, I told her I was
          unhappy in the relationship, and I was kind of—

LAURA   *(mimicking ROB)* —Looking around for someone
          else.

ROB VO   —Sort of maybe looking around for someone
          else. Did I do and say these things?

LIZ   NO!

LAURA   Yes.

          *LIZ springs to her feet. LAURA takes her hand
          and sits her back down.*

INT. GREEN MILL.

ROB   Did I do and say these things? Yes, I did. I did
          and said those things. I am a fucking asshole.
          But before you judge, although you've probably
          already done so, let me give you a top five: what
          are the top five worst things that you have done
          to your partner, even if – especially if – your part-

ner doesn't know about them. Don't dress things up or try to explain them. Just write them down in the plainest language possible...

EXT. GREEN MILL. NIGHT.

ROB emerges, comes up to the camera, checking his watch.

ROB   Pencils down. Okay, so who's the asshole now?

EXT. FANCY LINCOLN PARK TOWNHOUSE. DAY.

ROB mounts the stairs and rings the doorbell. The door opens, revealing a too-tan WOMAN in her late forties. She says nothing.

ROB   You called about the records?

INT. FANCY LINCOLN PARK TOWNHOUSE. DAY.

He follows through a fabulous first floor, packed with big-bucks bourgeois booty: rugs, art, and antiques.

She ushers ROB into a large study, and turns the light on. He misses a breath. The walls are lined with mahogany cases custom-built for thousands of CDs and albums – every one bagged and bearing a little numbered sticker, like a museum. She points to several boxes on the floor, full of hundreds of singles.

WOMAN   Those.

> *ROB, in awe, drops to his knees to examine the singles: the original 'God Save The Queen' by the Sex Pistols, original Otis Reddings, Elvis Presleys, James Browns, Jerry Lee Lewises, Beatles... on and on. The mother lode. ROB is doing his best to control the onset of hyperventilation.*

WOMAN *(cont'd)* What do you think?

ROB   It's the best collection I've ever seen.

WOMAN   Give me fifty bucks and they're all yours.

> *ROB's face goes funny. He looks around for a hidden camera.*

ROB   These are worth at least, I don't know—

WOMAN   I know what they're worth. Give me fifty and get them out.

ROB   But you must have—

WOMAN   I must have nothing. They're my husband's.

ROB   And you must not be getting along too well right now, huh?

WOMAN   He's in Jamaica with a twenty-three-year-old. A
        friend of my daughter's. He had the fucking nerve
        to call me and ask me to sell his singles collec-
        tion and send him a check for whatever I got,
        minus a ten-percent commission. Which reminds
        me. Can you make sure you give me a five? I
        want to frame it and put it on the wall.

ROB   It must have taken him a long time to get them
        together.

WOMAN   Years. This collection is as close as he's ever
        come to an achievement.

        *ROB looks back at the records but avoids the
        trance.*

ROB   Look. Can I pay you properly? You don't have to
        tell him what you got. Send him forty-five bucks
        and blow the rest. Give it to charity. Or some-
        thing.

WOMAN   That wasn't part of the deal. I want to be poison-
        ous but fair.

ROB   *(looking back at the records)* Look... I... I'm sorry.
        I don't want to be any part of this.

WOMAN   Suit yourself. There are plenty of others who will.

ROB   That's why I'm trying to compromise. What about fifteen-hundred? They're worth ten times that.

WOMAN   Sixty bucks.

ROB   Thirteen-hundred.

WOMAN   Seventy-five.

ROB   Eleven-hundred. That's my lowest offer.

WOMAN   And I won't take a penny over ninety dollars.
          They start smiling at each other.

ROB   I'm sorry, but I think you better talk to someone else.

WOMAN   Fine.

          ROB half stands, then drops again for one last lingering look.

ROB   Can I buy this Otis Redding single off you?

WOMAN   Sure. Ten cents.

ROB   Oh, come on! Let me give you ten dollars.

WOMAN   Okay. Because you took the trouble to come up here. And because you've got principles. But that's it. I'm not selling them to you one by one.

CUT TO

EXT. ARMITAGE STREET STATION. DAY.

> *ROB crosses the road toward the station. He pauses outside waiting for the camera to catch up with him.*

ROB First of all: the money I borrowed from Laura. She had it and I didn't, and she wanted to give it to me.

> *FLASHBACK.*

> *LAURA and ROB. LAURA is trying to put a check in ROB's hands, who keeps nervously waving it off. Finally he accepts.*

ROB VO If she hadn't, I would have gone under. I've never paid her back because I've never been able to...

EXT. ARMITAGE STREET STATION. DAY.

> *ROB enters the station and walks up the stairs.*

ROB ...And just because she's took off and moved in with some Supertramp fan doesn't make me five grand richer. Number two: the stuff about half looking around for someone else: she tricked me into saying it. We were having this state-of-the-union-type conversation and she said, quite matter-of-factly, that we were pretty unhappy at the moment, and did I agree, and I said yes, and she asked whether I ever thought about meeting someone else.

INT. EL TRAIN. DAY.

ROB sits, rocking slightly with the movement of the train. An OLD COUPLE who do not speak to each other sit across from him.

ROB   I asked her if she ever thought about it, and she said of course, so I admitted that I daydream about it from time to time. Now I see that what we were really talking about was her and Ian, and she suckered me into absolving her. It was a sneaky lawyer's trick, and I fell for it, because she's much smarter than me. Then the pregnancy. I didn't know she was pregnant. Of course I didn't. She hadn't told me. She hadn't told me because I had told her I had... sort of... slept with somebody else. So – I didn't find out she was pregnant 'til way later.

EXT. STREET. DAY. FLASHBACK.

ROB and LAURA walking down the street, talking. He says something, and she stops, beginning to weep. He turns and notices she's not next to him, and goes to her. She shakes him off, but then turns into his arms.

ROB VO   We were going through a good period and I
         made a crack about having kids and she burst
         into tears. I made her tell me what it was all
         about, and she did, and then I went into a brief
         and ill-advised bout of self-righteousness – my
         child too, what right did she have, blah blah
         blah—

EXT. WICKER PARK. DAY.

ROB and LAURA sit on a bench.

LAURA   You were fucking somebody else at the time,
         Rob, so you didn't really seem like a very good
         long-term bet. There didn't seem to be much of a
         point in consulting you about it.

EXT. TRAIN. DAY.

*The train begins to slope downward from above
the street and into the mouth of the subway tun-
nel.*

INT. TRAIN. NIGHT.

ROB   I guess that pretty much brings us up to date...
         (thinks) Who needs a drink?

         CUT TO

ROB IN HIS CHAIR.

> *On his third Hamms in a can, digging through a*
> *box, fishing through pictures and letters, concert*
> *tickets, old address books and other mementos.*
> *He begins to assemble a small pile.*

ROB   What is wrong with me? What happened to me?
Seriously – why am I doomed to be left?
He flips through a tattered old high-school date-
book with a big Rolling Stones lips logo peeling
off it and comes to what he's looking for.

ROB *(cont'd)* I need answers. Number one: Alison Ashmore.

> *He puts his finger on the page and dials the*
> *phone...*

INT. THE ASHMORES'. NIGHT.

> *A pleasant middle-class family's kitchen. Mrs*
> *Ashmore (ALISON'S MOM) watches an infomer-*
> *cial on a countertop TV while she goes through a*
> *stack of bills. The phone rings.*

ALISON'S MOM   Hello?

ROB IN HIS CHAIR. INTERCUT.

ROB   Hello. This is Rob Gordon calling. An old friend of
Alison's. Is, uh—

ALISON'S MOM'S brow furrows as she listens.

ALISON'S MOM   What did you say your first name was?

ROB   Rob. Rob Gordon. Alison's first boyfriend. I'm wondering—

ALISON'S MOM   I hate to quibble with you, Rob. She married her first boyfriend. Kevin Bannister. That's her first and last boyfriend.

ROB   You gotta be kidding me.

ALISON'S MOM   No, I'm quite serious. She's Mrs Kevin Bannister. She lives in Australia.

ROB   In the seventh grade we went out together.

ALISON'S MOM   Kevin's her first boyfriend. She's not in seventh grade anymore.

ROB   Technically, I'm her first boyfriend, okay? I went out with her for three days before Kevin did. Her first boyfriend. Me.

ALISON'S MOM   Okay. Well, I don't know what you mean by technically number one, but... maybe it's my mistake. I have to go, Bob... Goodbye.

She hangs up the phone and sits there for a beat. She looks at her watch, calculating, then picks up the phone.

CUT TO

INT. ROB'S APARTMENT. NIGHT.

> *ROB puts down the phone. He raises his hands up in the air.*

ROB   Married her junior-high sweetheart... Kissed me on the bench, kissed Kevin on the bench... married Kevin. What chance would I have had against that? None, no chance. Alison married Kevin. That's fate. That's destiny. Beyond my control, beyond my fault.

> *He drops down into the couch and begins rifling through the pile of scraps, which is now on the coffee table.*

ROB *(cont'd)* I want more. I want to see the others on the Big Top Five. I'd like to call up Penny, Charlie, all the people and ask them how they are and whether they've forgiven me, and tell them that I have forgiven them. Like a Bruce Springsteen song. And say good luck, goodbye.

BRUCE SPRINGSTEEN *(to camera)* No hard feelings.

ROB   And then they'd feel good and I'd feel good.

BRUCE SPRINGSTEEN   We'd all feel good.

ROB   I'd feel clean, and calm.

BRUCE SPRINGSTEEN   And ready to start again! Hey,
          that'd be good!

ROB   Great even.

INT. RECORD STORE. BACK ROOM. DAY.

> *ROB holds an old crumpled address book in one
> hand and the phone in the other.*

ROB   *(into phone)* Penny Hardwick? This is Rob
          Gordon... From high school... Yeah... No, you
          too... yeah...

INT. MUSIC BOX THEATRE. NIGHT.

> *ROB and PENNY sit in a movie theatre, looking
> quite comfortable together.*

ROB VO   Penny is as beautiful as she was in high school,
          and really grown into herself. She reviews movies
          for a living, which is unassailably cool. Even if she
          does make notes with this little flashlight pen.

EXT. MUSIC BOX THEATRE. NIGHT.

> *ROB and PENNY walk out of the theatre mid-conversation. They look happy as they walk down the street.*

INT. STREGA NOTA. NIGHT.

> *A mid-scale trattoria. ROB and PENNY sit at a table laughing and talking. If we didn't know better we might think there is chemistry.*

ROB VO   She tells me about her life... And I tell about mine... We both get it and we both relate...

CLOSE UP – ROB talking.

ROB VO   *(cont'd)* ...And then, with no real explanation, I just launch into it. I tell her about how Laura wanted to sleep with Ian and not me, Charlie wanted to sleep with Marco and not me, Alison Ashmore wanted Kevin Bannister and not me—

ROB   ...and even you wanted to sleep with Chris Thompson and not me, and... and I thought you could help me understand why it keeps happening...

> *He slows to a stop. We see PENNY as she goes from happy to livid.*

PENNY   Rob. I was crazy about you. I wanted to sleep
          with you, one day, but not when I was sixteen.
          When you broke up with me – when *you* broke up
          with *me* – because I was, to use your charming
          expression, tight, I cried and cried and I hated
          you. And then that little shitbag asked me out,
          and I was too tired to fight him off, and it wasn't
          rape because I said okay, but it wasn't far off.
          And I didn't have sex with anyone else until after
          college because I hated it so much. And now you
          want to have a chat about rejection? You're
          insane, Rob.

          PENNY stands and leaves. ROB just sits.

ROB   My God. She's right! I did break up with her. I
          rejected her! *(Cheerful)* So that's another one I
          don't have to worry about. I should have done
          this years ago.

          ROB indicates to an off-screen waiter.

ROB *(cont'd)* Check...

INT. APARTMENT CLOSET. NIGHT.

          ROB is on his knees, going through a box.

ROB   Next up, Charlie... but I don't think I'm quite
          ready for that. So I go directly to number four on
          the all-time break-up list. Sarah, my partner in
          rejection who rejected me.

INT. APARTMENT BUILDING HALLWAY. NIGHT.

*ROB's point of view of a door opening, revealing
SARAH, a few years older but still pretty in her
mousy way. She looks at ROB with a bit too
much in her eyes.*

ROB VO   She's easy to find. She sends me a Christmas
card every year from the same address that says
nothing.

INT. HI RICKY. NIGHT.

*ROB and SARAH face each other over a half-
eaten pizza.*

SARAH   I can't believe I left you for him... Crazy.

*SARAH looks down at her plate, shaking her
head, blushing. ROB looks uncomfortable. This is
more than he was looking for.*

ROB   Well... probably seemed like a good idea at the
time.

She looks up again...

SARAH   Probably. I can't remember why, though.

... and back down again.

73

ROB VO   I haven't got the heart for the rejection conversation. There are no hard feelings here, and I am glad that she ditched me, and not the other way around.

INT./EXT. APARTMENT BUILDING HALLWAY. NIGHT.

SARAH, in the doorway, smiles painfully. It's clear she doesn't want to shut the door, but she does. ROB turns and walks down the hall toward the door to the street as he talks to camera.

ROB   I could've ended up having sex back there. And what better way to exorcise rejection demons than to screw the person who rejected you, right? But you wouldn't be sleeping with a person. You'd be sleeping with a whole sad single-person culture. It'd be like sleeping with Talia Shire in *Rocky* if you weren't Rocky. I already feel guilty enough as it is... There's only Charlie left now.

INT. ROB'S APARTMENT. MORNING.

CLOSE-UP: phone book as ROB's finger moves down the column, then stops.

ROB VO   She's in the fucking phone book.

He dials.

ROB VO *(cont'd)* She should be living on Neptune. She's an extraterrestrial, a ghost, a myth, not a person in the phone book... I left my name and number and threw in a 'long time no see...' She doesn't call back.

INT. RECORD STORE. DAY.

Saturday. For the first time we see the place kind of busy. ROB watches the room. BARRY is toward the back, talking to a CUSTOMER. 'Cruel To Be Kind' by Nick Lowe plays.

BARRY   It's almost impossible to find, especially on CD. Yet another cruel trick on all of the dumbasses who got rid of their turntables. But every other Echo and the Bunnymen album—

CUSTOMER   I have all of the others.

BARRY   Oh really. Well what about the first Jesus and Mary Chain?

CUSTOMER   They always seemed...

BARRY   They always seemed what? They always seemed really great, is what they always seemed. They picked up where your precious Echo left off, and you're sitting here complaining about no more Echo albums. I can't believe that you don't own that record. That's insane.

*He plucks it from the rack, and sticks it in the
CUSTOMER's hand, who regards it with a bit of
shame.*

*DICK is listening to a FEMALE CUSTOMER,
ANNA, but he doesn't hear her voice.*

*FEMALE CUSTOMER – DICK's point of view. The
army bag with a red cross on it. The ring-of-ivy
tattoo around the wrist. The monkey boots. The
eye shadow.*

DICK thinking, calculating...

DICK   The interesting thing about Green Day is that so
            much of their music is in truth directly influenced
            by, in my opinion, two bands.

FEMALE CUSTOMER   The Clash.

DICK   Correct. The Clash. But also the Stranglers.

FEMALE CUSTOMER   Who?

DICK   I think you would love the Stranglers...

            *DICK pulls a Stranglers record and puts it on the
            stereo. Her brow furrows, and then she smiles.*

FEMALE CUSTOMER   This sounds great.

DICK smiles humbly. Uncomfortable geek chemistry seems to be happening with DICK and this girl.

FEMALE CUSTOMER *(cont'd)* My name's Anna.

DICK   Name's my... My name's Dick.

Two people in the store turn and approach.

CUSTOMER   Is this the new Green Day?

DICK shrugs humbly to her.

BARRY is still talking to his CUSTOMER, who now has several CDs in his hand. He looks at BARRY with a mixture of hate and adoration.

BARRY   That is perverse. Do not tell anyone you don't own fucking *Blonde on Blonde*. Do you have indoor plumbing?

BARRY adds more records to the customer's stack.

A few minutes later – ROB and DICK stand behind the counter. ROB holds a CD in his hand, and surveys the roaming customers with a semiserious air of authority.

ROB   I will now sell four copies of *Accelerator* by the Royal Trux.

DICK   Do it. Do it.

ROB pops the CD in and it begins to play... He stands there with his arms folded, waiting. After a moment, a customer approaches.

CUSTOMER   *(re: music)*   What is this?

ROB   It's the Royal Trux.

CUSTOMER   It's great.

ROB   I know.

ROB'S point of view of the room. Something has caught his eye: a cropped head with a leopard skin pattern surfaces and disappears, like Nessie.

ROB's face gets hot and mad. He jumps out from behind the counter. He moves like a cat through the crowd. VINCE and JUSTIN bolt for the door. ROB doubles back.

ROB *(cont'd)*   DICK! THE DOOR!

DICK sees VINCE and JUSTIN too late. ROB is right behind them and as they get out the door, he reaches... and comes up with the back half of a skateboard.

EXT. RECORD STORE. DAY.

> *ROB emerges behind them, VINCE's skateboard
> in hand. They have enough distance to bolt, but
> they can't leave that board behind.*

ROB   Okay, fuckos. How much is this deck worth to
you, and how many CDs did you rip off? Can you
do the math?

> *JUSTIN pulls two CDs out and slides them over
> to ROB.*

ROB *(cont'd) (to Vince)* And what about you, dork?

> *VINCE pulls about six, and puts them down in a
> neutral spot. ROB picks all of them up and starts
> looking through them. DICK pokes his head out
> of the door.*

ROB *(cont'd)* Dick, call the police, please.

> *VINCE and JUSTIN look at each other.*

ROB *(cont'd) (looking through the CDs)* Eno import. Sigue
Sigue Sputnik. Break Beats. Serge Gainsbourg.
Ryuchi Sakamoto... What's going on here? Are
you guys stealing for other people now?

VINCE   Naw. Those are for us.

ROB   Oh really. You two are slamming to Joni Mitchell
           now?

JUSTIN   You're, like, so bigoted to look at us and, like,
           think you know what we listen to.

VINCE   You got the CDs so can I have my board back?

ROB   I think you have more.

           *JUSTIN reaches down again into his baggy shorts
           and comes up with a tattered old book,* How to
           Make a Recording. *He tosses it over.*

ROB *(cont'd)* Jesus. That thing's been in the bargain bin for
           six months! Was it just your criminal nature, or
           what?

JUSTIN   We don't know how it works. Nobody even
           knows, so we wanted to check it out in that mag.

           ROB snorts.

VINCE   Like, do you know how to actually make a CD?

           *ROB can't resist edifying them – the curse of the
           underappreciated expert.*

ROB   Uh, yes I, like, do know how to make a record.

VINCE   Records are those big round black things, right?

ROB   Fuck off.

           ROB drops the skateboard and enters the store.

           CUT TO

INT. RECORD STORE. NIGHT. QUICK CUTS.

           *BARRY emerges from the back with three
           opened bottles of beer as the last customer goes
           out the door... The three lean against the bins,
           tired and smiling.*

ROB VO At the end of the Saturday, I have a little glow on,
           maybe because this is after all my line of work
           and it's going OK...

DICK   We rang $900 today.

ROB VO ...maybe because I'm proud of us, of the way
           that, though our talents are small and peculiar,
           we use them to the best advantage.

EXT. RECORD STORE. NIGHT.

           *ROB, now alone, turns the sign from 'open' to
           'closed', shuts the door behind him, and pulls the
           gate across. LAURA appears from the next door-
           way.*

LAURA   I thought I could give you a lift back.

ROB   Are you coming home?

LAURA   Yes. Well, I'm coming over to your house to get
           some things.

ROB   My house?

           LAURA turns and begins walking.

LAURA   How'd it go today?

ROB   Alright.

LAURA   Well, you look like you had a good day.

ROB   I did. But this isn't exactly a feel-good period of
           my life.

           CUT TO

INT. ROB'S APARTMENT. NIGHT.

           *The lock turns and ROB enters, holding the door
           for LAURA who slips by, her coat in her hands.
           He picks up IAN's envelope and hands it to her.*

ROB   You can take it with you if you want.

Above: Record shop owner Rob (JOHN CUSACK) and soon-to-be-ex-girlfriend Laura (IBEN HJEJLE).

Below: Barry (JACK BLACK), Dick (TODD LOUISO), Rob and singer Marie De Salle (LISA BONET) in Championship Vinyl.

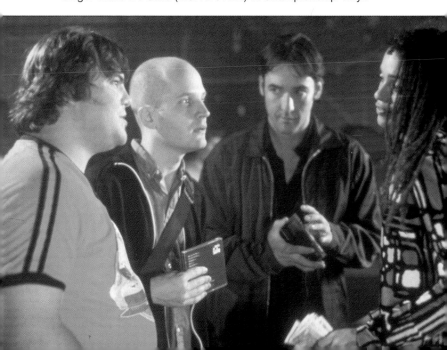

Above: Rob struggles with his self-examination of life's most baffling issue: love.

Below: Rob and Dick try to discuss their feelings.

Above: Rob and Sarah (LILI TAYLOR).

Below: Jo (JILL PETERSON), Rob and his sister Liz (JOAN CUSACK).

Left:
Wannabe rock star Barry's performance surprises everybody.

Below: Rob takes a walk.

Laura and Rob before the split.

Above: A couple for eight years, Laura and Rob have an extensive back-catalogue of memories.

Below: A younger Rob takes a look at his reflection.

Above: Rob, the respectable owner of Championship Vinyl.

Below: Rob provides some invaluable customer service.

Above: Rob begins to fall for the sultry singer Marie De Salle.

Below: Rob meets up with Penny (JOELLE CARTER), another of his ex-girlfriends.

She slips it into her purse. He stands facing her for a moment, then crosses to her, takes her coat and tosses it on a chair. She opens the closet and takes out a big laundry sack.

LAURA   Have you tackled the Great Reorganization yet?

ROB   You bet.

She begins putting books and other things into the bag...

ROB *(cont'd)* Look at this place. What're you making now, sixty, seventy grand a year? And you were living in this dump?

LAURA   I was here because I wanted to be with you. It had nothing to do with this place.

ROB   So where are you staying now?

LAURA   I think you know that.

ROB   Had to work it out for myself, though, didn't I?

LAURA looks suddenly tired and sad, and looks away.

LAURA   I'm sorry. I haven't been very fair. That's why I came to the store tonight. But it took me a while to work up the courage.

ROB   Are you scared now?

LAURA   Yes, of course I am. I feel terrible, Rob. This is
           really hard, you know.

INT. BEDROOM. CLOSE UP. ROB

ROB is sitting in bed, facing us.

ROB   I want to tell her I'm sorry for everything, and I
           love her, and I miss her, and have you missed me
           at all, even one bit, do you love me? do you love
           him? when did you start seeing him, and was it
           because of the ceiling-noise thing? and is this
           really definitely it, or just some sort of phase?
           and do you want to have babies with him, and is
           it better, is it better, IS IT BETTER!

           CUT TO

THE APARTMENT

ROB   So. Is it working out with Ian?

LAURA   Rob. Don't be childish.

ROB   You're living with the guy! I'm just asking how it's
           going.

LAURA   I am not living with him. I've just been staying
         with him for a few days until I work out what I'm
         doing. Look, this has nothing to do with anyone
         else. I left because we weren't exactly getting
         along, and we weren't talking about it. I'm getting
         to a point where I want to get my shit together
         and I can't really see that ever happening with
         you, and yeah, I sort of got interested in some-
         one else, and that went further than it should
         have, so it seemed like a good time to go. But I
         have no idea what will happen with Ian in the
         long run. Probably nothing.

         *LAURA, her bag half filled with clothes, goes to
         the bookshelves next to the records. She starts
         topping off the bag with books.*

ROB   So, what, you haven't definitely decided to dump
         me? There's still a chance we'll get back together.

LAURA   I don't know.

ROB   Well, if you don't know, there's a chance, right?
         It's like, if someone was in the hospital and he
         was seriously ill and the doctor said, I don't know
         if he's got a chance of survival or not, then that
         doesn't mean the patient's definitely going to die,
         now does it? It means he might live. Even if it's
         only a remote possibility.

LAURA   I suppose so.

ROB   So we have a chance of getting back together
           again.

LAURA   Oh, Rob, shut up.

ROB   Hey, I just want to know where I stand. What
           chance—

LAURA   — I don't fucking know what chance you fucking
           have!

           She abandons her attempt at packing.

ROB   Well if you could tell me roughly it would help.

LAURA   Okay, okay, we have a nine percent chance of
           getting back together. Does that clarify the situa-
           tion?

ROB   Yeah. Great.

LAURA   I know I'm asking a lot, but will you take off for a
           while so I can get my stuff packed up?

ROB   No problem. If I can ask one question.

LAURA   Fine. One.

ROB   You won't like it.

LAURA   Just ask it!

ROB   Is it better?

LAURA   Is what better? Better than what?

ROB   Well. Sex, I guess. Is sex with him better?

LAURA   Is that really what's bothering you?

ROB   Of course it is.

LAURA   You really think it would make a difference either
        way?

ROB   I don't know.

LAURA   Well the answer is that I don't know either. We
        haven't done it yet.

ROB   Never?

LAURA   I haven't felt like it.

ROB   But not even before, when he was living
        upstairs?

LAURA   No. I was living with you, remember? We've slept
        together but we haven't made love. Not yet. But
        I'll tell you one thing. The sleeping together is
        better.

ROB   *(trying not to smile)* The sleeping together is bet-
             ter but not the sex because you haven't done it
             with him yet.

LAURA   Will you please just go?

ROB   Good.

             *A long uncomfortable silence as they stare into
             each other's eyes.*

EXT. STREET. NIGHT.

             *ROB bounces along, a smile wider than we have
             seen yet. Maybe even jumping to touch an
             awning. He lands and tells us:*

ROB   I feel good! I feel great! I feel like a new man. I
             feel so much better, in fact – that I go straight out
             and sleep with Marie.

INT. MARIE'S BEDROOM. DAWN.

             MARIE is asleep in bed. ROB beside her awake.

ROB   How does he do it? – you ask.

             *He gingerly gets out of bed and pulls on his jeans
             and T-shirt, making his way toward the couch.*

ROB *(cont'd)* How has a regular guy like me become the Number One Lover Man in this particular district? 'He's grumpy, he's broke, he hangs out with the Musical Moron Twins, and he gets to go to bed with a real-life recording artist.'

INT. RAINBO CLUB. NIGHT.

> *ROB enters, still grinning a bit like a proud new father. He scans the room and sees the table where BARRY, DICK, and MARIE sit. He goes to them and sits in the empty seat, next to MARIE. The boys nod his way, and continue talking. MARIE turns to him.*

MARIE   Everything go alright?

> *ROB glances at BARRY, who averts his gaze.*

ROB   She just wanted to pick up some stuff. No big thing.

MARIE   God, I hate that time. The pick-up-stuff time. That's what 'Eartha Kitt Times Two' is about. Me and my ex dividing up our record collections.

ROB   It's a great song.

MARIE   Thank you.

ROB   Is that why you're in Chicago? Because of, you know, dividing up your record collection and stuff?

MARIE   Yup.

INT. MARIE'S LIVING ROOM. DAWN.

ROB   Awhile back, Dick and Barry and I agreed that
         what really matters is what you like, not what
         you are like. Books, records, films – these things
         matter.

INT. RAINBO CLUB. NIGHT.

         ROB and MARIE talk.

ROB   Wait, who was it?

BARRY   McGoohan. Patrick McGoohan.

         *They all laugh. MARIE slides closer, turning her
         back on the others – the loop is closed.*

INT. MARIE'S LIVING ROOM. DAWN (CONT'D).

ROB   Call me shallow, but it's the damn truth, and by
         this measure I was having one of the best dates
         of my life. References, titles, lyrics, flew and met
         each other in mid-air embraces. The evening
         goes with breathtaking precision.

INT. RAINBO CLUB. LATER (CONT'D).

> *ROB and MARIE, on a couch, lean intimately into each other.*

ROB Then we talk about our exes. She's honest, with a self-deprecating sense of humour, and I can see why her songs are so good. I don't talk about Laura with as much depth, but it feels, even to me, like I'm being intimate. I express regret, I say nice things about her, and I hint at a deep melancholy just below the surface. But it's all bullshit really. I've just invented a sketch of a decent, sensitive guy.

INT. MARIE'S APARTMENT. NIGHT.

> *ROB leans on a table. MARIE drops ice in two glasses.*

MARIE You know, I really thought you hated me. You were always so odd when I was around.

ROB Is that why you were interested?

MARIE Yeah, kind of I guess.

ROB That's not the right answer.

MARIE No, but... if a guy's kind of weird with me, I want to find out what's going on, you know?

She comes back from the kitchen and faces him.

ROB   And you know now?

MARIE   Nope. Do you?

ROB   Nope.

            *She turns to him and runs her fingers through his
            hair.*

MARIE   I'd like it if you'd stay the night.

ROB   Oh. Well—

            *She leans into him, and they begin to kiss. ROB's
            eyes stay open.*

            CUT TO

INT MARIE'S LIVING ROOM. DAWN.

            ROB sits on the couch.

ROB   Why is failure the first thing I think about?
            Sometimes I wish I were my old man. He never
            had to worry about making mom's all-time hot
            one hundred, because he was first and last on
            the list.

INT. LIVING ROOM. NIGHT.

> *A well-appointed, unpretentious living room, with the otherworldly plainness of a TV stage. ROB sits in an easy chair. Pull back to reveal ROB'S DAD, in a comfy sweater sitting on the couch across from ROB, smiling.*

ROB   Dad, did you ever have to worry about the female orgasm? Do you in fact know what a female orgasm is? Do you envy me my sex life, or does it all look like hard work to you?

ROB'S DAD Listen, son. The good fuck wasn't even invented in my day. By the time I saw a girl naked, I had already married her. So, stop whining and get on with it.

BACK TO MARIE'S APARTMENT. NIGHT (CONT'D.)

ROB   Yeah. Sure. I'll stay.

MARIE   Good.

           *MARIE kisses him deeply and takes him by the
           hand, leading him toward the bedroom.*

INT. MARIE'S LIVING ROOM. DAWN.

           ROB on the couch.

ROB   And then we make love, and it's great, and that's
           it. I'm not going to go into all that other stuff, the
           who-did-what-to-whom stuff. You know 'Behind
           Closed Doors' by Charlie Rich? That's one of my
           favourite songs... You're entitled to know that we
           had a good time.

           *MARIE enters and sits down beside ROB on the
           couch.*

MARIE   What're you doing?

ROB   Thinking.

MARIE   Me too.

ROB   Work anything out?

MARIE   Little bit. I've worked out that I was real lonely, and I went to bed with the first person who'd have me. And that I was lucky it was you, and not somebody mean, or boring, or crazy.

ROB   I'm not mean, anyway. And you wouldn't have gone to bed with anyone who was any of those things.

MARIE   I don't know. I had a bad week.

ROB   Me too.

MARIE   I could tell. And I wasn't fooled by you acting all cool about... what's her name?

ROB   Laura.

MARIE   Laura, right.

ROB   What was yours called?

MARIE   It was called James.

ROB   Do you miss him?

MARIE   Sure. That's the way it works, right?

         She laughs a little, and so does he.

MARIE *(cont'd)* I don't know. I think people are allowed to
feel horny and fucked-up at the same time.
(beat, smile)
Why should we be denied our basic human rights
just because we've messed up our relationships?

ROB laughs.

ROB   You think sex is a basic human right?

MARIE   You bet. And I'm not gonna let that asshole stand
between me and a fuck.

ROB   *(smiling)* That's a pretty intense thing to say.

MARIE   Yeah, I guess it is.

EXT. MARIE'S APARTMENT. MORNING.

*ROB and MARIE come out of the building and
into the street.*

ROB   Which way are you going?

MARIE *(points left)* That way. You?

ROB *(points right)* That way.

MARIE   And so it is. I'll talk to you later.

They smile at each other.

96

ROB   I'll call you.

MARIE   Right.

           ROB and MARIE set off down the street, in the
           different directions.

ROB   What did Laura mean last night, she hasn't slept
           with him yet? Yet. What does 'yet' mean, any-
           way? What does that mean? It means you're
           going to, doesn't it? Or does it?

INT. IAN'S APARTMENT. MORNING.

           LAURA sleeps next to IAN, who strokes her hair.
           He is scruffier than ROB, and looks not unlike Leo
           Sayer/Steve Guttenberg. She wears sweatpants
           and a T-shirt. He seems to be nude.

IAN   *(whispers)* Laura? Laura?

           Her eyes open and she turns to him. He kisses
           her softly on the mouth.

           She kisses him back, tentatively and with open
           eyes. She backs up and looks at him, then away,
           considering. He begins to smile.

INT. RECORD STORE. NEXT DAY.

*Empty. ROB leans against the register talking to
BARRY who is playing a Game Boy, the room
behind them. DICK prices records at the other
end of the store.*

BARRY just looks at ROB.

ROB   Just... come on, what would it mean to you? That
        sentence? 'I haven't seen *Evil Dead II* yet?'

BARRY   To me, it would mean that you're a liar. You saw it
        twice. Once with Laura – oops – once with me
        and Dick. We had that conversation about the
        possibilities of the guy making Baretta shotgun
        ammo off-screen in the fourteenth century.

ROB   But say I hadn't seen it and I said to you, 'I
        haven't seen *Evil Dead II* yet,' what would you
        think?

BARRY shuts the Game Boy off.

BARRY   I'd think you were a cinematic idiot. And I'd feel
        sorry for you.

ROB   No, but would you think, from that one sentence,
        that I was going to see it?

BARRY   I'm sorry, Rob, but I'm struggling here. I don't
         understand any part of this conversation. You're
         asking me what I would think if you told me that
         you hadn't seen a film that you've seen. What am
         I supposed to say?

ROB   Just listen to me. If I said to you—

BARRY   —I haven't seen *Evil Dead II* yet, yeah, I hear
         you—

ROB   Would you... would you get the impression that I
         wanted to see it?

BARRY   Well... you couldn't have been desperate to see
         it, otherwise you'd have already gone...

         ROB brightens.

ROB   Right! She's not going to see that movie!

         BARRY finally considers.

BARRY   ... But the word 'yet...' Yeah, you know what, I'd
         get the impression that you wanted to see it.
         Otherwise you'd say you didn't really want to.

ROB   But in your opinion, would I definitely go?

BARRY   How the fuck am I supposed to know that?
         Probably!

ROB darkens.

ROB   Why?

BARRY   Because it's a brilliant film. It's funny, violent, and the soundtrack kicks fucking ass.

They look at each other for a strange moment.

BARRY *(cont'd)* I never thought I'd say this, but can I go work now?

INT. LAURA'S OFFICE. AFTERNOON.

LAURA, on the phone, frustrated as hell.

LAURA   I'm at work...

INT. RECORD STORE. BACK ROOM. INTERCUT

ROB is curled up with the phone.

ROB   If you don't want me to call you at work then just give me your home number. I'm sorry, Laura, but I'm not going to put the phone down until you've agreed to meet up for a drink. I don't see why things should be on your terms all the time.

LAURA whips her pen across the room.

LAURA   Okay, okay, okay, okay, okay. Tonight. Come
          down and get me at the office.

ROB   Tonight? Friday? Really? You're not busy? Great.
          It'll be—

          She hangs up—

ROB *(cont'd)* —nice to see you.

INT. LAURA'S OFFICE. LATE AFTERNOON.

          *LAURA packs a few things into her briefcase. LIZ
          sits on the sofa with her feet up.*

LIZ   Where is this sudden well of desperate love com-
          ing from? Why in hell does he want you back?

          LAURA gives LIZ a look.

LIZ *(cont'd)* No, I mean, why now?

LAURA   Because I'm with someone else first. That's it.
          And if I went back—

LIZ   —He'd eventually meet someone and leave you.

LAURA   That's what I'm thinking. Maybe it's worth going
          back for two weeks and let him do the breaking
          up.

LAURA pulls her coat off of a hook and puts it on.

LIZ   That's sad.

LAURA   I know.

LIZ   And depressing. Mmn. Well. How's Ian?

LAURA   He's growing on me.

LIZ   He looks like he could grow on something.

EXT. OFFICE BUILDING. LATE AFTERNOON.

ROB stands under the overhang, watching LAURA walk toward him down the long hallway from the elevators to the door.

ROB VO   She looks different. Something has happened, maybe something real, or maybe something in her head. Whatever it is, you can see that she thinks she's started out on some new stage in her life. She hasn't. I'm not going to let her.

She looks up and sees ROB outside – she stops in her tracks.

INT. DOWNTOWN BAR. LATE AFTERNOON.

Populated by the happy-hour crowd of business-people. ROB and LAURA have just sat down in a booth.

LAURA   So, how are you?

ROB   Have you slept with him yet?

LAURA   Is that why you wanted to see me?

ROB   I guess.

LAURA   Rob. What do you want me to say?

ROB   I want you to say that you haven't, and I want it to be the truth.

She looks past him.

LAURA   I can't do that.

She starts to say something else, but ROB is up and out. 'I Want You' by Elvis Costello begins to play...

EXT. DAMEN AVENUE. NIGHT.

> *It has started to rain. ROB pushes through the rush-hour raincoats, seeming to be the only one going his way.*

INT. ROB'S APARTMENT. NIGHT. INTERCUT.

> *ROB is soaking. The phone rings. He pulls off his headphones and picks it up but says nothing.*

INT. IAN'S APARTMENT. INTERCUT.

LAURA   You must have known it would happen. You couldn't have been entirely unprepared. Like you said, I've been living with the guy. We were bound to get around to it sometime.

> *She laughs nervously. ROB says nothing.*

LAURA *(cont'd)* Rob. Are you there? What are you thinking?

ROB   *(barely a whisper)* Nothing.

LAURA   We can meet for another drink if you want. So I can explain it better. I owe you that much.

ROB   How much would be too much?

LAURA   Will you call me?

ROB   I don't have your number.

LAURA   Call me at work. We can arrange to meet properly.

ROB   Okay.

LAURA   Because I don't want this to be the last conver-
          sation we have. I know what you're like.

ROB   You do, huh.

          ROB hangs up and stares at the wall for a while.
          LAURA clicks the phone off and exhales. She
          turns around to find IAN in the doorway, a pot in
          one hand and a wooden spoon in the other, held
          out for her to taste a sauce. She starts.
          ROB gets a beer from the fridge and sits back
          down. He picks up the phone and dials.

ROB *(cont'd)* Yes, a residence, a Mr Ian Raymond, North
          Side... thank you.

          He writes down a number and hangs up. He
          picks up the phone and dials. Hangs up. Picks
          up, dials. He hangs up quickly—

          CUT TO:

EXT. IAN'S APARTMENT. NIGHT.

> *It's still raining. ROB is tucked into a phone booth across the street. He picks up the phone, drops a quarter, and hits the numbers hard as he dials... a muffled male 'hello?' is heard and ROB hangs up. He does it again. And again. And again. Until —*

INT. IAN'S APARTMENT. INTERCUT.

> *Still an unpacked box or two, but it's set up: a framed* Woodstock – The Movie *poster, a bread maker – you get the idea. IAN stares at LAURA with amused exasperation. She picks up the phone—*

ROB   I just wanted to say that I think you're running from a point that everyone hits in any relation- ship, and you're just going to hit it again with Ian but it's going to be later, when you're older, and with this idiot who doesn't really understand you, not the way I do and will even more in the future.

LAURA   Hold on...

> *She walks into another room, shutting the door behind her. On a bookshelf is a picture of a younger IAN in a tunic, emoting on some college stage.*

ROB   I mean, if you want to experiment, or whatever—

She turns the picture face down and wanders over to the window, looking out absently.

EXT. IAN'S APARTMENT. INTERCUT.

Rain. She sees ROB down there at the phone booth.

LAURA   *(indignant)* I'm not experimenting. Why don't you go experiment.

INT. IAN'S APARTMENT. INTERCUT.

IAN OS   *(through the door)* Laura? Are you okay?

LAURA   *(covering the mouthpiece, to IAN)* I am fine...
(to ROB) I gotta go. Call me at work. Goodbye.

She clicks the phone off. The door cracks and IAN sticks his head in.

IAN   You look upset.

LAURA   I'm upset, but I'm fine.

IAN   Maybe I should talk to him.

LAURA   Mmmm, no. Not a good idea.

IAN   Conflict resolution is my job, Laura.

> *She grabs her coat and opens the door. The phone begins to ring.*

LAURA   *(waving toward the door)* Nothing to resolve, Ian. Let's get a drink. C'mon, c'mon.

EXT. IAN'S APARTMENT.

> *ROB stands on the sidewalk in the rain. His head turns at the sharp sound of a door opening — IAN and LAURA are coming out of the building. He jumps behind a tree, peering around it as they fade down the street.*

ROB   *(pointing down the street)* Two blocks down on Webster here? The garage where the St Valentine's Day Massacre took place. They should rename this neighborhood Betrayal Town.

> *CUT TO*

INT. GREEN MILL. NEXT NIGHT.

> *ROB and LIZ sit.*

LiZ   You've got to stop calling her. You're really upsetting her. And him.

ROB   Oh, like I care about him.

LIZ   Well you should.

ROB   Why?

LIZ   Because all you're doing is forming a little unit,
        them against you. Before you started all this
        psychotic behaviour there was no unit. There
        were just three people in a mess. And now
        they've got something in common, and you don't
        want to make it any worse.

ROB   How could it get any worse than Laura with Ian?
        That stupid fucking laugh! That cause-of-the-
        month lefty hip bullshit politics and the—

LIZ   Rob. Let me ask you a question. You can think
        about it if you want.

ROB   Just what is it?

LIZ   Why do you want her back so badly?

ROB   Why do you think?

LIZ   I have no idea. Laura doesn't either.

ROB   Well if she doesn't then what's the point?

        She wickedly demurs.

LIZ   I've seen men like you in movies but I never
           thought they existed in real life. *(Affected voice)*
           The man who can't commit, who can't see the
           point. *(Drops the voice)* But here you are. A living,
           breathing specimen. Incredible.

INT. ROB'S APARTMENT. NIGHT.

           *ROB sits at the kitchen table, drinking a beer and
           listening to music coming from the other room.*

ROB VO   Top five things I miss about Laura. One. Sense of
           humour. Very dry... caustic without being cruel,
           but it can also be warm and forgiving. And she's
           got one of the best all-time laughs in the history
           of all-time laughs. She laughs with her whole
           body. Two: She's got character, or at least had
           character before the Ian nightmare. She's loyal
           and honest, and open and curious. And she
           doesn't toy with chumps, even though chumps
           deserve it. And she doesn't take it out on other
           people even when she's having a bad day. That's
           character. Number three: I miss her smell, and
           the way she tastes. It's the mystery of human
           chemistry, and I don't understand it. Some peo-
           ple, as far as your senses are concerned, just...
           feel like home. Four: I really dig how she walks
           around. It's like she doesn't care how she looks,
           or what she projects. It's just that she has too
           much character to bullshit about it. She's not
           affected, I guess, and that gives her grace.

Number five: She does this thing in bed when she can't get to sleep. She kind of half moans and then rubs her feet together. It kills me. These are the top five reasons I love and miss Laura. Believe me, I could do a top five things about her that drive me crazy, but it's that kind of thinking that got me here.

INT. RECORD STORE. DAY.

ROB, in a foul mood, prices records, hitting them with the sticker gun with a bit too much force.

BARRY   Rob! Phone!

He goes through the door to the stockroom and picks it up.

ROB   Yeah.

INT. CHARLIE'S HOUSE. DAY. INTERCUT.

CHARLIE   Bonjour Rob Gordon!

ROB   Uh... Charlie?

CHARLIE   I just got back into town – Los Angeles for a seminar. So! Wow! Rob Gordon! The Rob Gordon! Seems like a hundred million years ago now.

ROB   Yeah. A billion. Right... So. How are you? Do you
           have, you know, kids and stuff, like everybody
           else?

CHARLIE   No, I'm too young, too single. I don't know, kids
           are too... time-consuming, I guess, is the expres-
           sion I'm looking for.

ROB   *(to us)* I'm not making this up. This is how she
           talks, as if nobody has ever had a conversation
           about this in the entire history of the world.

CHARLIE   I'm real busy.

ROB   Yeah.

CHARLIE   Real busy too?

           He looks around at his surroundings.

ROB   Yeah, sure. I'm fine... Got the store. Lotsa pro-
           jects.

CHARLIE   That's great... You are fine and you deserve to be
           fine. So anyway, are you in or out, Rob?

ROB   I'm sorry.

CHARLIE   It's just... I find these long-lost boyfriend calls a
           little unnerving. There's been a rash of them,
           recently.

ROB   Is that right?

CHARLIE Well, do you remember that guy Marco I went out
         with after you?

ROB   Kinda.

CHARLIE Well, he called a few months back and I think he
         was going through some kind of 'what-does-it-
         all-mean' thing, and he wanted to see me, and
         rehash the past as they say, and I wasn't really
         up for it. Do all men go through this?

ROB   I've never heard of it before. What does 'are you
           in or out' mean?

CHARLIE It means, I don't know, are we friends or aren't
         we. So are you in or out?

ROB   I'm in.

CHARLIE Good. Do you want to come to a dinner party
         tomorrow night?

INT. RECORD STORE. DAY.

           *ROB comes out of the back. There's someone
           running his hands across the stacks — it's IAN.
           ROB reacts, gunfighter eyes.*

ROB   Can I help you?

IAN   Hello, Rob. Remember me? I'm Ray. Ian.

           ROB says nothing.

IAN *(cont'd)* I thought maybe we should talk. Sort a few
           things out...

ROB   What needs sorting out?

IAN   Ten phone calls a night... hanging around outside
           my house...

ROB   Yeah, well, I've stopped all that now.

IAN   You were out there this morning.
           *ROB is disoriented on the way to angry. DICK
           and BARRY's ears perk up.*

IAN *(cont'd)* Obviously I know how special Laura is, and I
           know things can't be good for you at the
           moment. I'd hate it if I lost her. But I'd like to
           think that if she decided she didn't want to see
           me anymore, I'd respect that decision. Do you
           see what I'm saying?

ROB   Yeah.

IAN   Good. So shall we leave it at that then?

ROB   I dunno.

IAN   Think about it, Rob.

            CUT TO FANTASY

            ROB looking sure of himself, righteous.

IAN   Good. So shall we leave it at that then?

ROB   I've already left it, you pathetic rebound fuck!
            Now get your patchouli stink out of my store!

            IAN leaves, rattled.

            CUT TO FANTASY

            same thing.

IAN   Good. So shall we leave it at that then?

ROB   We won't leave it, Ian. Not ever.

            *ROB springs back toward IAN, but BARRY blocks
            his way. DICK helps hold ROB back.*

DICK   Don't do it, Rob!

BARRY   He's not worth it!

            *ROB reaches a pointed finger over BARRY's
            shoulder.*

ROB   Leave town. Leave the country, you little bitch, because you're gonna look back on walks by the house and ten phone calls a night as a golden age. Get ready, motherfucker.

IAN trips backward and scurries out the door.

CUT TO FANTASY

ROB, DICK and BARRY just beating the living shit out of IAN, Rodney King style. IAN lies on the floor trying to cover himself. DICK, already out of breath, breaks from the pack and jerks the air conditioner from the wall and hefts it over his head, preparing for the death blow. He smashes it over IAN's head.

CUT BACK TO REALITY

IAN   So shall we leave it at that then?

ROB   I dunno.

IAN   Think about it, Rob.

INT. CHARLIE'S HALLWAY. NIGHT.

A high and open corridor. ROB, a bottle of wine in hand, checking apartment numbers as he smooths his hair. He finds CHARLIE's and rings the bell... We hear the muffled sound of pricey

>   *heels getting louder, then the door opens to*
>   *reveal CHARLIE. She looks stunning.*

CHARLIE Hey, Jellybean!

>   *She turns and leads him into a sprawling designer-*
>   *renovated loft, complete with a huge granite*
>   *cooking island. Surrounding the island are pleas-*
>   *ant and wealthy-looking PEOPLE in their thirties,*
>   *ad-libbing about cooking techniques and season-*
>   *ings as they semi-professionally put together*
>   *architectural and ornate gourmet dishes.*

CHARLIE *(cont'd)* Rob, this is everybody. Everybody, this is
Rob.

EVERYBODY Hi!

ROB   Hi.

>   *They go back to it. ROB looks for a stool at the*
>   *island, but there are none empty.*

CHARLIE *(to a guest)* Careful with that tuna, Camilla, or it
won't hold the filo.

>   *ROB backs up a few steps and sits on the arm of*
>   *a chair. He pours himself a wine at the coffee*
>   *table and lights a smoke.*

ROB VO   I can see that I'm doomed to die a long, slow, suffocating death. And I try to figure out why... Of course there's envy...

He looks at their coats thrown across a sofa.

ROB VO *(cont'd)* Why isn't my life like this?

INT. CHARLIE'S DINING ROOM. SERIES OF SHOTS OVER THE COURSE OF DINNER.

The other guests talk and eat. ROB's central activities are working his way through maybe a few too many wines and making sure his cigarette smoke doesn't get in anyone's face. Highfalutin conversation about poetry, world politics, etc. intermingle with:

ROB VO   I want their money and clothes and jobs and opinions, and I'd like to have advice on jet lag. But that's not it... They're not bad people, and I'm not a class warrior, it's something else... And then it dawns on me... Charlie's... awful.

EXT. ROOFTOP DECK. LATER.

CHARLIE is kissing people goodbye as they leave. ROB, somewhat bleary, leans on a rail at the edge of the roof. After CHARLIE sees the last guest off, she notices ROB and crosses the roof toward him.

ROB VO   She doesn't listen to anyone, she says terrible stupid things, and she apparently has no sense of humor at all, she talks shit all night long... Maybe she's been like this all along. How had I managed to get it all wrong? How did I turn her into the answer to all of the world's problems?

ROB   Hey, Charlie.

CHARLIE Hey, Rob.

ROB   Why did you break up with me for Marco?

CHARLIE *(on her feet)* Fuck! I knew it! Fuck, fuck, fuck!

ROB   What?

CHARLIE You are going through one of those what-does-it-all-mean things.

ROB   I can't lie when I drink. I am, actually, yes. Yes, indeed. Very much so.

        She laughs at him.

ROB *(cont'd)* C'mon, answer the question. You can say what you like. What the hell? C'mon, why did you break up with me for Marco?

        CHARLIE looks off at a corner of the ceiling, musters a look of 'contemplation'.

CHARLIE *(sudden Irish accent)* It's all kind of lost in the... in the dense mists of time now.

She waves her fingers in front of her eyes, presumably to indicate mist, then drops the accent.

CHARLIE *(cont'd)* It wasn't that I really like Marco more. In fact, I thought you were more, shall we say, attractive than him. It was just that he knew he was good-looking and you didn't, and that made a difference somehow. You used to act as if I was weird for wanting to spend time with you, and that got me kind of beat, if you know what I mean. Your self-image started to rub off on me and I ended up thinking that I was strange. You made me laugh, and I dug the way you got consumed by things you loved... but Marco seemed a bit more, I don't know, glamorous? More sure of himself?

Pause.

CHARLIE *(cont'd)* Less hard work, because I felt like I was dragging you around, sort of.

Pause.

CHARLIE *(cont'd)* A little sunnier. Sparkier.

Pause.

CHARLIE *(cont'd)* I don't know. You know what people are
              like at that age. They make very superficial judge-
              ments. Do you think that's superficial?

ROB   On the contrary. Those are the first un-superficial
              words that have crossed your lips all night.

CHARLIE Aww. Did that hurt? He was a clown, if it's any
              consolation.

ROB   Did you tell him that?

CHARLIE Of course not. I didn't want to hurt his feelings.

            CUT TO

INT. RECORD STORE. DAY.

            FLYER ON THE WALL:
            'Hip young gunslingers wanted for new
            band/Must be into REM, Primal Scream, Fanclub,
            etc./Contact BARRY in the store/No slackers,
            please.'

ROCK GUY You put this ad up?

BARRY   That's right.

ROCK GUY What can you play?

BARRY *(proudly)* Nothing. What kind of stuff are you into?

ROCK GUY The kind of stuff you, you know, mentioned. But
we want to be more experimental than that. We
want to retain our pop sensibilities, but kind of,
you know, go a little further out there.

> *ROB and DICK listen. ROB rolls his eyes, DICK is
> frozen in concentration.*

BARRY   Sounds great.

ROCK GUY No gigs yet. We just got together. Is Tuesday
night cool with you? We'll just, you know, jam.

> *The ROCK GUY scribbles his info and hands it to
> BARRY.*

BARRY   Right. Fine.

ROCK GUY Okay. Later.

> *The ROCK GUY leaves. BARRY goes behind the
> counter and starts looking for a record. He stops,
> noticing ROB and DICK who stare at him.*

BARRY   What?

ROB   'What?' What do you mean, 'What?' You've had
that thing on the wall for fucking years and some
guy comes in, and... and you just act like it's no
big deal.

BARRY   It's just a fucking garage band. Nothing special.

ROB   But – you don't play an instrument!

BARRY   *(thinks)* I can sing... Do you think I'm going to
          stick around here all my life? Hey, it's seven
          o'clock. Let's go.

DICK   I... can't go to the club tonight, guys.

BARRY   Why?

          DICK smiles sheepishly.

BARRY *(cont'd)* Who are you going to see?

DICK   Nobody.

          BARRY's eyes widen.

BARRY   Rob, looky looky. Dick! Are you getting some?!

          Silence.

BARRY *(cont'd)* Un-fucking-believable. Dick's got a hot
          date! How did this happen, Dick? What rational
          explanation can there possibly be? What's her
          name?

          DICK shrinks back.

DICK   Anaugh.

BARRY   Anna who? Anna Green Gables? Anna Conda?

DICK   Anaugh Mass.

BARRY   And you met this bruiser where, exactly? A home for the mentally challenged, or for the blind? Or the bus station?

DICK   Um... here. On Saturday. She asked for the new Green Day, and then I told her—

BARRY   Finally! Anna! Good for you, Dick. Really. Smoke that ass.

         BARRY picks up his bag and heads for the door.

BARRY *(cont'd)* You know what, Rob? I can't go to the club either. *(Sighs)* I got some lyrics to get down on paper.

DICK   Yeah. Me too. Not lyrics to get down... Anaugh said that we... Okay. I'll see you tomorrow, Rob.

         DICK exits. ROB watches the door close behind him, suddenly alone. Outside he sees DICK cross the street to ANNA. They embrace clumsily/tenderly, and move off together. ROB goes to the light switches and shuts them down. ROB's silhouette slips out the door.

ROB   I have to do something about this place.

INT. ROB'S APARTMENT. NIGHT.

>   *ROB sits at the kitchen table, scribbling some-*
>   *thing on a piece of paper...*

ROB VO   Let it go, burn it down, whatever, and find myself
          a career.

INT. RECORD STORE. LATE MORNING.

>   *ROB, DICK and BARRY stand at the counter.*

DICK   So would a saxophonist and pianist count as two
           different jobs?

ROB   Yes.

BARRY   What about guitarist and bass player?

ROB   I don't know. Just one, I'd think.

BARRY   So Keith Richards had the same job as Bill
           Wyman, according to you? Someone should've
           told the Stones that, bro. It could've saved them
           a lot of trouble.

INT. ROB'S APARTMENT. NIGHT.

> *ROB opens his door to find LAURA sitting at the kitchen table, reading his piece of paper.*

ROB   Hey—

LAURA   *(reads)* Top Five 'Dream' Jobs.

ROB   That's private.

LAURA   Yeah, yeah, yeah. Number one: Journalist for *Rolling Stone* magazine, 1976–1979. Get to meet the Clash, Sex Pistols, Chrissie Hynde, David Byrne. Get tons of free records. Number two: Producer, Atlantic Records, 1964–1971. Get to meet Aretha, Wilson Pickett, Solomon Burke. More free records. And a shitload of money. Number three: Any kind of musician. Besides classical or rap. Settle for being one of the Memphis Horns, or something. Not asking to be Hendrix or Jagger or Otis Redding. Four: film director.

ROB   Yeah. Any kind. Except German. Or silent.

LAURA   And at number five we have architect.

ROB   I guess.

LAURA   Seven years' training.

He shrugs.

LAURA *(cont'd)* Are you prepared for that?

ROB   Not really.

LAURA   I didn't think so.

ROB   I'm not sure I really want to be an architect.

She smiles and sighs.

LAURA   So you've got a list here of five things you'd do if
         qualifications, and time, and history, and salary
         were no object, and one of them you don't really
         want to do anyway.

ROB   Well, I did put it in at number five.

LAURA   Wouldn't you rather own your own record store
         than be an architect?

ROB   I suppose.

         *LAURA scratches and scribbles on the page,
         hands it back to ROB.*

LAURA   Well there you are then. You might as well stick
         with the store. It comes in at number five in your
         list of dream jobs. Dream job number five.

It sinks in for a second, not unpleasantly. Then he snaps out of it.

ROB   I find it interesting that you keep showing up here.

LAURA   This is the last of it.

ROB   Those look heavy. Where's Ian? Or Ray? What is his fucking name?

LAURA   Ray. I hate Ian.

ROB   I hate him too.

They smile.

LAURA   I'm sure.

She stands and begins walking out.

LAURA *(cont'd)* See ya.

ROB   Hey. There's some CDs of yours over there. Take 'em if you want.

LAURA pauses at the record shelves and picks up a stack of ten or so CDs. She looks them over.

LAURA   Where's *Endless Summer*?

ROB   I didn't think you like that. I gave it to you
           because I wanted you to like it because I liked it,
           and that's kind of futile and stupid, so…

LAURA   Well I do like it.

ROB   You can take it. Or you can always just show up
           again tomorrow.

LAURA   Ha ha.

           She leaves.

EXT. CLARK STREET. DAY.

           *ROB comes down the street toward the store.
           VINCE and JUSTIN are doing skateboard tricks in
           the street. As ROB walks by VINCE's skateboard
           goes out from under him and careens into ROB's
           shin.*

ROB   AHHH. YOU MAGGOTS!

           He starts to take a run at them, but backs up.

INT. RECORD STORE. DAY.

           ROB limps into the store.

DICK   Laura called.

ROB   Thanks.

            *He heads toward the back but stops, looks up at
            a speaker... stopped for a moment by the music.*

ROB *(cont'd)* Hey, what's...

            *He turns to DICK and BARRY, who are staring at
            the tape deck like two concerned doctors, listen-
            ing to a song that is raw and moody and lyrical —
            Minor Threat meets Brian Eno, if that's possible.
            ROB joins them in contemplation at the counter.*

ROB *(cont'd)* What is this.

DICK   It's Vince and Justin.

ROB   Who's that?

BARRY   The little skate-fuckers.

ROB   No way.

BARRY   Yes way. It's really...

            ROB and DICK look at him, ready to pounce—

BARRY *(cont'd)* *(pained to say it)* It's really fucking good.

DICK and BARRY look to ROB, who continues to just listen... He takes a deep breath and walks to the front door and out, seemingly with a mission.

EXT. RECORD STORE. DAY. ROB, VINCE AND JUSTIN.

VINCE and JUSTIN are doing noisy skate tricks against the curb across the street. ROB comes out of the store and toward them followed by DICK and BARRY, who lurk in the background. VINCE and JUSTIN get ready to flee.

ROB   Your tape. It's good.

          They mumble thanks.

ROB *(cont'd)* It's rough. But it shows promise. I'll put out your record. Any profits after recouping expenses get split down the middle.

VINCE   Wait a minute. Island Records charged U2 a million five in expenses against their overhead for one plane ride.

ROB   We're not there yet, Justin.

VINCE   I'm Vince.

ROB   Whatever. What's the name of your band?

JUSTIN   The Kinky Wizards.

VINCE   We saw this ad in the personals for two swingers lookin' for a Renaissance fair.

ROB   Nice.

JUSTIN   What's the name of your label?

ROB   Top Five Records. Welcome aboard.

INT. RECORD STORE. DAY.

ROB walks back to answer the phone.

BARRY   WHAT THE FUCK WAS THAT! You just told them that you're gonna put out a record with them?

ROB   So? You even said they're good. What are you so hot about?

BARRY   Just that you seem to think it would be wiser to start a record label by putting out a record with business-crippling Nazi Youth shoplifters than with someone you know in your bitter jealous heart is a musical visionary. That's all.

ROB   Okay, Barry. What do your songs sound like? The Sex Pistols? Nirvana? The Smurfs?

INT. RECORD STORE. BACK ROOM. DAY.

ROB tosses his coat down in the storeroom and picks up the phone and dials...

BARRY   You probably wouldn't be familiar with our imme-
          diate influences.

ROB   *(in the doorway)* Try me.

BARRY   They're mostly German.

ROB   What? Kraftwerk? Falco? Hasselhoff?

          *He slams the door on the front room, picks up
          the phone, and dials.*

INT. IAN'S APARTMENT. INTERCUT.

LAURA OS *(muffled, almost a whisper)* Hello.

ROB   Hey, you called?

          No answer.

ROB *(cont'd)* Are you alright?

LAURA OS *(sniffling)* Pigsty.

ROB   Then come home. The place is spotless and I'll
          nurse you back to health.

LAURA OS Pig died.

ROB   Who the fuck's Pig?

133

LAURA OS *(louder)* My dad died. My dad, my dad.

> *She hangs up.*

INT. RECORD STORE. DAY.

> *ROB comes out of the back, in a daze. DICK and BARRY notice.*

BARRY   What's up?

ROB   Laura. Her dad died.

BARRY   Ooh. Drag.

DICK   I'm sorry, Rob, wow that's —

> *BARRY goes back to his comic book and burrito.*

ROB   You're a horrible person, Barry. I mean it.

> *BARRY looks up at him, shrugs, then gets an idea.*

BARRY   Hey. Top five songs about death. A Laura's Dad Tribute List.

> *Nobody can help thinking about it.*

BARRY   *(cont'd)* Okay, okay — 'Leader of the Pack'. The guy fucking cracks up on a cycle and dies right? 'Dead Man's Curve', Jan and Dean...

DICK   Did you know that after that song was recorded, Jan himself crashed his —

BARRY   —It was Dean, you fucking idiot.

ROB   *(as if dealing with children)* It was Jan, and it was a long time after—

BARRY   Whatever. Okay. 'Tell Laura I Love Her'. That'd bring the house down. Laura's mom could sing it.

The phone rings.

BARRY   *(cont'd)* I'd want 'One Step Beyond' by Madness. And 'You Can't Always Get What You Want'.

ROB   *(Answers the phone)* Championship Vinyl.

INTERCUT. IAN'S APARTMENT.

LAURA is curled up on the couch. DICK and BARRY keep listing.

LAURA   I'm sorry.

ROB   No, no. When are you going home?

LAURA   In a minute. When I get it together.

BARRY   *(to Dick)* What about Sabbath? Or Nirvana?
        They're into death.

        *ROB tries to signal them to shut up but they don't
        see him. He moves as far away as the cord will let
        him.*

ROB   Can I do anything?

DICK   'Abraham, Martin and John.' That's a nice one.

BARRY   'Bela Lugosi's Dead', Bauhaus. It's got that
        creepy Halloween feeling.

LAURA   No. No. Mom wants you to come to the funeral.
        It's on Friday.

ROB   Me?

LAURA   My dad liked you. And Mom never told him we'd
        split, because he wasn't up to it and... I don't
        really understand it. I think she thinks he'll be
        able to see what's going on. It's like... *(small
        laugh)* He's been through so much, what with
        dying and everything, that she doesn't want to
        upset him any more than she has to.

ROB   Do you want me to be there?

LAURA   I don't care. As long as you don't expect me to
           hold your hand.

           ROB is silent.

LAURA   *(cont'd)* Look, are you coming or not?

ROB   Yes, of course.

LAURA   Liz'll give you a lift.

           She hangs up.

BARRY   *(to the tune of 'Candle in the Wind')* Goodbye
           Laura's dad/blah blah la di da di da/ *(belting it
           out)* Seems to me/you lived your life/like a dentist
           in the wind...

           *ROB stomps toward BARRY, who jumps over the
           counter to keep singing—*

INT. CHAPEL TWO. LATE AFTERNOON.

           *ROB sits in the back of the dark, smallish nonde-
           nominational room. At the front is a coffin, resting
           on a stand. LAURA, her younger sister JO, and
           LAURA's MOTHER sit in the front row, listening to
           the MINISTER.*

MINISTER ...Now and forever, Amen.

> *He nods offstage, and a muffled mechanical noise is heard. The coffin begins to lower through a trapdoor beneath it. A low, baleful human howl is heard starting quietly but gaining in volume.*

ROB VO   I can only just tell that it's Laura's voice, but I know that it is, and at that moment I want to go to her and offer to become a different person, to remove all trace of what is me, as long as she will let me look after her and try to make her feel better.

INT. LAURA'S PARENTS' HOUSE. NIGHT.

> *A cozy old Victorian house. ROB and LIZ stand, drinking wine. LAURA is in the background dealing with other guests. Jo approaches them.*

LIZ   *(to Jo)* How are you?

JO   I'm all right, I suppose. And Mom's not too bad. But Laura... I dunno.

LIZ   She's had a pretty rough few weeks already, without this. It's hard when you're putting all your efforts into one part of your life and it doesn't work out.

> *She glances at ROB, embarrassed.*

ROB   *(sincere)* Don't mind me. No problem. Just pre-
           tend you're talking about somebody else.

           JO smiles, LIZ gives him a look.

LIZ   We are talking about somebody else. Laura.

           *Rob begins to turn red. Anger, sorrow, everything
           else building.*

ROB   Enough, Liz.

LIZ   Enough of what?

ROB   *(Getting louder)* You know, Liz, I can either stick
           up for myself or believe everything you say about
           me and end up hating myself. And maybe you
           think I should, but it's not much of a life, you
           know? I'm really sorry, Jo.

LIZ   Maybe I've been a little unfair. But is this really
           the time?

ROB   Only because it's never the time. I can't go on
           apologizing my whole life, you know?

LIZ   I have to say that just the once would do.

           ROB looks around the room...

Across the room, LAURA is consoled by a guest.

GUEST   I'm sorry, Laura.

ANOTHER GUEST I'm so sorry, Laura.

ROB appears in front of her.

ROB   I'm sorry.

He slips out the room. She watches him until another guest approaches her. She slips away herself, up the stairs.

EXT. LAURA'S PARENTS' HOUSE. NIGHT.

Raining, ROB emerges and begins to walk down the street...

INT. BATHROOM. NIGHT.

LAURA looks at herself in the mirror for a long minute. She exhales, tension slipping away, something settled.

EXT. SUBURBAN STREET. NIGHT.

Raining torrents and big sheets. ROB walks down the street, hands thrust into his pockets. The rain almost immediately soaks him.

EXT. LAURA'S PARENTS HOUSE. NIGHT.

> *LAURA's car leaves the house.*

EXT. SUBURBAN STREET. NIGHT.

> *ROB comes to a bus stop bench and takes a seat. Down the street, ROB notices LAURA's car turn the corner toward him. He vaults himself over a small brick wall and into a flower bed, landing on his back in the black wet earth. The big drops of rain splash mud on his face, and he burrows deeper into the dirt. Off-camera the car engine catches up, and comes to a stop. He sighs and shuts his eyes, listening to the idling engine. After a long beat he sits up and looks over the wall. LAURA, sitting in her car, rolls down the window and motions him toward her.*

LAURA   Are you going to lie in that flower bed all night?

ROB   Uh... no.

> *He gets up, brushes his muddy self off, and steps over the wall and to the car.*

LAURA   You're soaking.

ROB   Mmmn.

LAURA   You're also an idiot.

ROB   I know. Look, I'm sorry. I really am.

LAURA   Thank you. I appreciate it.

ROB   I don't want to take up any more of your time.
           You get back. I'll wait here for the bus.

LAURA   I don't want to be there... that isn't the way I
           want to mourn my father. When Liz told me you'd
           left I used it as an excuse to get out.

ROB   Anything I can do.

LAURA   Let's go.

ROB   ... Where?

LAURA   I'll show you. C'mon.

*He pulls himself up and starts to climb over the
fence.*

INT. LAURA'S CAR. NIGHT.

*LAURA's car pulls up in a quiet place, a field in
front of an old abandoned school.*

LAURA   Dad used to bring us here when we were kids.

ROB just listens.

LAURA   *(cont'd)* Listen, Rob, would you have sex with
          me?

ROB   I'm sorry?

LAURA   I want to feel something else than this. It's either
          that or I go home and put my hand in the fire.
          Unless you want to stub cigarettes out on my
          arm.

ROB   I've only got a couple left. I'm saving them for
          later.

LAURA   It'll have to be sex then.

          *ROB looks himself over: ill-fitted suit, soaking wet
          and dirty. He looks like he just dragged himself
          out of a garden.*

LAURA   *(cont'd)* I knew there was a reason I wore a skirt
          today. Just stay there.

          *She pulls herself over him, straddling him in the
          passenger seat and kissing his neck. She pauses
          and regards him from above.*

LAURA   *(cont'd)* Hello. It doesn't seem so long ago that I
          looked at you from here.

ROB   Hi.

> LAURA *reaches down and unzips his pants, as*
> *they keep kissing.*

ROB   *(cont'd)* ... Are you still on the pill?

LAURA   Yes, of course. There's nothing to worry about.

ROB   I didn't mean that. I mean... with Ray... was that
        all you used?

> LAURA *looks at him, motionless, then begins to*
> *cry.*

ROB VO Is Ray bisexual or an intravenous drug user? I
        doubt it. The truth is, I wasn't really worried about
        where he's been. I just wanted to hurt her, on this
        day of all days, just because it's the first time
        since she left me I've been able to...

> *He starts to wipe away her tears. He takes her in*
> *his arms. He kisses her tenderly.*

EXT. LAURA'S PARENTS' HOUSE. NIGHT.

> *ROB and LAURA pull up in front. In the front win-*
> *dow we can see LAURA'S MOTHER, pacing.*

LAURA   I'm too tired. I'm too tired not to go out with you.
        Maybe another time I would have the guts to be
        on my own, but not now I don't.

ROB   What about Ian?

LAURA   Ray's a disaster. I don't know what that was all
        about. I know it's not very romantic, but there will
        be romance again at some stage, I'm sure. And it
        was me who wanted you at the funeral, not my
        mom. It never occurred to me to invite Ray, and I
        felt so tired and I missed you so much, and you'd
        made it clear you wanted me back, so...

        *She looks out the window. Her MOTHER stares
        daggers from the distance.*

LAURA *(cont'd)* Shit. Hold on.

        *LAURA gets out of the car and walks toward the
        house.*

        CUT TO

INT. ROB AND LAURA'S APARTMENT. LATE MORNING

        *They sleep, both on their backs, hands clasped in
        unconsciousness. The sun takes one more move,
        cutting through the sill and crossing ROB's eyes,
        bringing them open. He looks over at her, then
        back at the ceiling, smiling. She rolls into his
        chest and opens her eyes...*

LAURA   Can you not go to work today?

ROB   (gestures at the clock) I'm already not at work
             today.

             She smiles and kisses his side.

LAURA   Good.

             They begin to make love. He stops.

ROB   So... with Ian. What was it like good sex or was it
             like bad sex?

LAURA   Look, Rob. If great sex was as important as you
             think it is, and if I was having great sex with him,
             then we wouldn't be lying here right now. And
             that is my last word on the subject, okay?

ROB   Okay.

EXT. PARK. DAY.

             *Flea market in progress – plywood racks of
             records and blankets with old tools and crap –
             behind ROB and LAURA, who are walking toward
             us. He holds a stack of records, she holds one,
             an Art Garfunkel album.*

ROB   How can you like Art Garfunkel and Marvin
             Gaye? It's like saying you support the Israelis and
             the Palestinians.

LAURA   It's not like saying that at all, actually Rob. Art
         Garfunkel and Marvin Gaye make pop records—

ROB   —Made. Marvin Gaye is dead, his father shot him
         in—

LAURA   —Whatever, and the Israelis and the Palestinians
         don't. Art Garfunkel and Marvin Gaye are not
         engaged in a bitter territorial dispute, and the
         Israelis and Palestinians are.

ROB   Alright, alright.

LAURA   Who says I like Marvin Gaye, anyway?

         He reels on her.

ROB   Hey! Marvin Gaye! 'Got to Give it Up!' That's our
         song! Marvin Gaye is responsible for our entire
         relationship!

LAURA   Is that right? I'd like a word with him.

ROB   You remember?

LAURA   I remember the song. I just couldn't remember
         who sang it.

         ROB shakes his head in disbelief.

ROB   You used to care more about things like that.

When I first met you and I made you that tape you loved it. You said – and I quote – 'It was so good it made you ashamed of your record collection.'

LAURA   Well, I liked you. You were a DJ, and I thought you were hot and I didn't have a boyfriend, and I wanted one.

ROB   So you weren't interested in music at all?

LAURA   Yeah, sure. But I was more interested in you.

           She loops her arm through his and gets him moving again.

INT. ROB'S KITCHEN. NIGHT. MONTAGE.

           ROB and LAURA having a late-night conversation over the kitchen table, punctuated with laughter and closeness.

ROB VO   So we got back together and we had a great time and we talked and listened and we had fun...

INT. ROB'S BEDROOM. NIGHT. MONTAGE.

           ROB and LAURA making love.

ROB VO   ... And we had great sex all the time and that was terrific and then wouldn't you know it?

> *ROB stops the love-making and gets out of bed,*
> *entering the bathroom.*

ROB   Suddenly I feel panicky, and sick, and I want to
        run around and sleep with female recording
        artists...

INT. RECORD STORE. DAY.

> *Close-up: very pretty young woman, CAROLINE,*
> *smiling.*

CAROLINE Excuse me? What's that playing?

ROB   It's Mouse On Mars.

CAROLINE It's great.

ROB   I know. I love that mouse.

CAROLINE Is your name Bob?

ROB   It's Rob.

CAROLINE Riiight. Yeah, Rob. You used to be a DJ. I used
        to go to the Dodger to hear you spin. You were...
        unbelievable. My name's Caroline.

ROB   Huh. You used to come to the club? You must
        have only been about sixteen.

ROB realizes what he must be sounding like. He blushes.

CAROLINE So is this your store?

ROB   Yeah. Uh, what do you do?

          She points to a stack of free Readers *by the door.*

CAROLINE I work for the *Reader*. I write a music column.

          His eyes light up.

ROB   That's... Oh! You're Caroline Fortis.

BARRY   Rob? Phone!

ROB   *(over his shoulder)* Take a message.

BARRY   It's your girlfriend!

ROB   *(to CAROLINE)* Excuse me.

          He goes to the phone.

ROB   *(cont'd)* Hi.

LAURA   Listen, do you want to go to dinner at Paul and
          Miranda's? Paul from work.

ROB   Oh. Well. We don't really get along. Paul and I.

LAURA   I know. But I'm thinking maybe it's just because
          you've never met. It just seems like a stone
          unturned in your relationship with him.

ROB   Ha.

          CUT TO

          INT. PAUL AND MIRANDA'S DINING ROOM.
          NIGHT. MOS.

          ROB and LAURA sit with PAUL and MIRANDA.
          They seem to be having a great time, and ROB,
          despite himself, is having a good time.

ROB VO   And though I try to fight it, I sort of fall in love
          with Paul and Miranda – with what they have,
          and the way they treat each other, and the way
          they make me feel as if I'm the new center of
          their world.

EXT. PAUL AND MIRANDA'S BACK PORCH. NIGHT.

          ROB pulls off a cigarette, standing on a small
          square of planking behind an old brownstone.
          Behind him we see LAURA, PAUL and MIRANDA
          through a picture window, finishing dinner at a
          table inside.

ROB   I think they're great, and I want to see them twice a week, every week, for the rest of my life. Only later do I realize I've been set up.

LAURA joins him on the porch.

LAURA   Rob. Go and look at their records.

ROB   I don't have to. I am capable of surviving without turning my nose up at other people's record collections, you know.

LAURA   Please, I want you to.

INT. PAUL AND MIRANDA'S LIVING ROOM. LATER.

After dinner, ROB ambles in from the dining room. He looks through the bookshelves until he finds a meager little grouping of CDs. He moves up to them and scans the titles: Tina Turner, Billy Joel, Kate Bush. Pink Floyd. Celine Dion. The Titanic *soundtrack. Simply Red. The Beatles. The Windham Hill sampler.*

PAUL   Lame, right?

ROB turns around to see PAUL behind him.

ROB   Oh, I don't know. The Beatles are okay.

PAUL laughs.

MIRANDA We're kinda out of date.

ROB   Hey, to each his own, I say.

LAURA   'To each his own!' Unbelievable! You! Rob
         Gordon said that. You even sounded like you
         meant it.
ROB   I did mean it. What?

         CUT TO

EXT. STREET. NIGHT.

         As ROB and LAURA walk home. ROB is pissed.

ROB   You did that deliberately. You knew all along I'd
         like them. It was a trick.

LAURA   I tricked you into meeting some people you'd
         think were great. I thought it would be fun to
         introduce you to someone with a Tina Turner
         album and then see whether you still felt the
         same way. Everybody's faith needs testing from
         time to time.

ROB   What are you talking about?

EXT. MILWAUKEE AVENUE. MORNING.

> ROB walks to work, drinking his coffee... He
> stops and backs up a few feet, and stares at a
> poster on a plywood board-up.

> 'I SOLD MY MOM'S WHEELCHAIR/the debut
> single from The Kinky Wizards/on Top Five
> Records/Record Release Party July 20 at Double
> Door/Featuring the triumphant return of DJ ROB
> GORDON/Dance Music For Old People.'

> The color drains from him. He picks up the pace.

INT. RECORD STORE. LATE MORNING. BOYS DREAM JOBS.

> DICK and BARRY unbox records. ROB enters.

ROB   What the hell is this?!!

BARRY   Talk to your woman.

DICK   Her idea...

> He points to the same poster, now on the wall.

ROB   Oh, Christ...

INT. APARTMENT. NIGHT.

> *ROB paces in front of LAURA. She does all she can do not to laugh.*

ROB   'Dance music for old people?'

LAURA   Yeah... I had the idea when I was with Ian and it was such a good one that I was annoyed that we weren't back together anymore. It may be why I came back.

ROB *(incredulous)* A record-release party?

LAURA   You're releasing a record.

ROB   And now because of you everyone's going to fucking hear it.

> *LAURA laughs.*

ROB *(cont'd)* What if I was doing something that couldn't be cancelled?

LAURA   Rob! What are you ever doing that can't be cancelled? Oh. Guess what? Barry said his band'll play a set.

> *ROB wheels on her—*

INT. RECORD STORE. NEXT DAY.

ROB and BARRY.

ROB   Look. I'll give you ten per cent of the door if you don't play.

BARRY   We're getting that anyway.

ROB   Okay, twenty per cent.

BARRY   No. We need the gig.

ROB   A hundred and ten per cent. That's my final offer.

BARRY   We're called SDM. Sonic Death Monkey.

ROB   Sonic Death Monkey.

BARRY   What do you think? Dick likes it.

EXT. MILWAUKEE AVENUE. DAY

VINCE fails at doing tricks on a ramp of broken plywood. ROB and JUSTIN talk.

JUSTIN   Let me get this straight, dude. We made the CD with you, your friends and your girlfriend want to throw a party or something to, like, celebrate it or whatever, and you're asking us not to do it.

ROB   Exactly.

           JUSTIN's brow furrows and he thinks hard.

ROB   *(cont'd)* What?

JUSTIN   That just seems kind of, I don't know... fucking
           stupid. I mean, what's the big deal, dude?

           ROB doesn't have a comeback for this truth.
           JUSTIN begins to walk toward the ramp.

JUSTIN   *(cont'd)* I don't get invited to parties very often.
           I'm goin'.

VINCE   *(calls out)* Me too.

           ROB turns and walks away.

INT. APARTMENT. NIGHT.

           ROB enters to find LAURA sitting on the couch.
           He flops down next to her with a sigh.

ROB   From whichever angle I look at it, it still looks like
           you did this just because you love me. So thanks.

           She takes his hand.

LAURA   You made something. The critic, the professional
           appreciator put something new into the world.

The second one of those things gets sold to
somebody, you're officially a part of it.
Congratulations, Rob.

She smiles. He doesn't.

ROB   Right.

LAURA   It hurts, doesn't it?

ROB   Yes.

ROB (cont'd) I'm sorry I've been acting like a jerk. And I do
          love you, even though I act like I don't.

LAURA   That's okay. You seem so moody all the time
          though.

ROB   I know. I just don't get it.
          *He kisses her and smiles. She goes into the bed-
          room. ROB looks at the poster.*

INT. RECORD STORE. DAY.

          CAROLINE enters and beelines to ROB.

CAROLINE Rob! What's the Kinky Wizards thing? I wanna
         do a story on it.

ROB   Story on what? It's just a three-song EP by a
           couple of burgeoning criminals.

CAROLINE You're DJ-ing again and you're putting out a
         record, and it'll be sort of a then-and-now story
         against the backdrop of the Chicago music
         scene.

ROB   Mmmn.

CAROLINE So. Is now a good time to ask you a few ques-
         tions?

                 *ROB looks around: there is absolutely nothing
                 going on in the store. He nods. She pulls out a
                 pad and pencil.*

CAROLINE *(cont'd)* You must have an enormous record col-
         lection.

ROB   Yeah. I could show it to you if you want to come
           over and see it.

                 He winces immediately.

CAROLINE Yeah, well... let's see... What are your all-time
         top five records?

ROB   Oh boy... In the club, or at home?

CAROLINE Is there a difference?

ROB   Of course. 'Sin City' by the Flying Burrito
             Brothers is an all-time top five, but I wouldn't
             play it at the club. It's a country-rock ballad.
             Everybody'd go home.

CAROLINE Nevermind. Any five. So four more.

ROB   What do you mean, four more?

CAROLINE Well if one of them is this 'Sin City' thing —

ROB   Can I go home and work this out and let you
             know? In a week or so?

CAROLINE Look, if you can't think of anything, it doesn't
             matter. I'll do one. My five favorite from the old
             days at the Dodger.

             ROB is aghast, humiliated, quietly outraged.

ROB   Oh, I'm sure I can manage something... 'Sin City'.
             'New Rose,' by The Damned. 'Hit It and Quit It'
             by Funkadelic. 'Shipbuilding,' Elvis Costello –
             Japanese import, no horns, or different horns
             anyway... um... 'Mystery Train' by Elvis Presley...
             and... 'Spaced Cowboy' by Sly and the Family
             Stone. A bit controversial, I know, but...

CAROLINE Fine, that's great.

ROB   Is that it?

CAROLINE That's five. Do you want to change anything?

ROB   *(Almost to himself)* 'Summertime Blues.' Blue
          Cheer version.

CAROLINE You want to put it in?

ROB   I'd better.

CAROLINE Okay, now – 'Music for Old People.' What does
         that mean?

ROB   Look, I'm sorry about this, but I'd like 'The
          Upsetter' by Lee 'Scratch' Perry, in there. Instead
          of 'Sin City.'

CAROLINE And the new label? And the Kinky Wizards?

ROB   The Kinky Wizards are – you know what? Why
          don't I just make you a tape?

          CAROLINE smiles.

INT. ROB AND LAURA'S APARTMENT. NIGHT.

          ROB and LAURA eat take-out.

LAURA   I don't believe it. How could you?

ROB   What?

LAURA   Ever since I've known you you've said 'Chantilly
         Lace' by Jerry Lee Lewis was the greatest
         recording of all time, and now it doesn't even
         make your top five?

ROB   Shit. Fuck. Fuck.

LAURA   And where the hell is Moby Dick—

ROB   —Moby Grape, 'Omaha.' Jesus you're right,
         you're right–

LAURA   And the Minutemen and the Zombies and Skip
         Spence and...

EXT. PAY PHONE. NIGHT.

         ROB tries to mask his urgency.

ROB   Yeah, Caroline, it's me. Again. It's Rob. I just
         wanted to leave you another song, um, I'm think-
         ing I already left you the Jerry Lee Lewis
         'Chantilly Lace' message, and I like that, love
         that, but it's kind of obvious and Gene Vincent's
         'Summertime Blues' is kind of overlooked, prob-
         ably because he spent so much time overseas –
         anyway, so 'Summertime Blues'...

INT. ROB AND LAURA'S APARTMENT. DAY.

ROB sits Indian-style on the floor in front of the stereo, hard at work making a tape.

ROB   The making of any compilation tape is a subtle art. Many do's and don'ts. You're using someone else's poetry to say what you feel, but you're always hiding behind the fact that it's someone else's poetry. So – first song – *(holds up a CD)* I'm thinking...

LAURA walks in the door behind him, sees him making the tape. He doesn't see her. LAURA turns and walks out the room.

ROB pulls the tape out of the stereo and taps it against his knee, thinking... His enthusiasm pales. He heaves an exhausted sigh and gets to his feet.

ROB *(cont'd)* When is this going to fucking stop?

ROB drops the tape into the trash.

LAURA   When's what going to stop?

ROB   Huh?

LAURA   *(re: tape)* Who's that for?

ROB   Oh, just the woman who interviewed me for the *Reader*.

EXT. PARK. TWILIGHT.

> *ROB walks by himself on the edge of the park.*

ROB   So should I just jump from rock to rock for the rest of my life until there aren't any rocks left? Should I bolt every time I get that feeling in my gut when I meet someone new? I've been thinking with my guts since I was fourteen years old and I've come to the conclusion that my guts have shit for brains.

> *CUT TO*

INT. RAINBO CLUB. DAY.

> *ROB sits at a table in the bar, nervous. He watches the door, sits up straight when it opens, and follows someone with his eyes, all the way to his table. She sits. It's LAURA.*

LAURA   A drinking lunch on a school day. What a nice surprise.

> *ROB says nothing.*

LAURA *(cont'd)* Are you worried about tomorrow night?

ROB   Not really.

> *He plays with his drink.*

LAURA   Are you going to talk to me, or shall I get my
         paper out?

ROB   I'm going to talk to you.

LAURA   Right.

         He plays with his drink some more.

LAURA *(cont'd)* What are you going to talk to me about?

ROB   I'm going to talk to you about whether you want
         to get married or not. To me.

LAURA   Ha ha ha. Hoo hoo hoo.

ROB   I mean it.

LAURA   I know.

ROB   Oh, well, thanks a fucking bunch.

LAURA   I'm sorry. But two days ago you were in love with
         that girl from the *Reader*, weren't you?

ROB   Not in love, exactly, but...

LAURA   Well forgive me if I don't think of you as the
         world's safest bet.

ROB   Would you marry me if I was?

LAURA   No. Probably not.

ROB   Right. Okay, then.

LAURA   What brought all this on?

ROB   I don't know.

LAURA   I'm just curious about how one goes from making
         tapes for one person to marriage proposals to
         another in two days. Fair enough?

ROB   I'm just sick of thinking about it all the time.

LAURA   About what?

ROB   This stuff. Love and marriage. I want to think
         about something else.

LAURA   I've changed my mind. That's the most romantic
         thing I've ever heard. I do. I will.

ROB   It's... I just... I mean, there've been others, all the
         time, and I have these fantasies and they seem
         great because there're never any problems, and if
         they are they're cute problems, like giving each
         other the same present for Christmas or she
         already went to see a movie with her friends that
         I want to see with her, and then I come home and
         you and I have real problems and you don't even
         want to see the movie I want to see, period,
         and... there's no lingerie, and—

LAURA   I have lingerie.

ROB   I know you do. You have great lingerie. But you
          also have cotton underwear that's been washed
          a thousand times and they don't. I mean, they
          do, of course, but I don't have to look at it
          because it's not in the fantasy. But I'm tired of the
          fantasy because it just doesn't exist. And there're
          never really any surprises, and for another, it
          never really...

LAURA   Delivers?

ROB   Right. Delivers. And I'm tired of it. And I'm tired
          of everything else, for that matter. But I don't
          seem to get tired of you.

LAURA   I think I know what you mean. But were you really
          expecting me to say yes?

ROB   I dunno. Didn't think about it, really. It was the
          asking that was the important thing.

          *She leans over and takes his hands in hers,
          smiles at him.*

LAURA   Well, you asked. Thank you.

INT. DOUBLE DOOR. NIGHT.

Two turntables with the mixer in the middle. 'Just Begun' by Jimmy Castor spins on turntable. A hand reaches in, and begins to draw the slides down, quieting the music.

ROB looks up from behind the DJ table, set up among the instruments. The place is packed with people, and everyone seems to be having a great time. Almost everyone – ROB sees BARRY, who pretends to nod off when ROB catches his eye, and JUSTIN, who looks back at him and mocks a bulimic act. ROB gives him the finger. He sees LAURA, and she beams at him. He comes to the front of the stage, and taps a microphone.

ROB   Uh, thanks for uh, coming out tonight. I hope you have a good time. And I hope you like the record. The one by the Kinky Wizards. The record that we're having this record-release party for. *(hoots from the crowd)* Thanks. Listen to it first, though. *(laughs)* Okay, we'll get to that later. Right now, I'd like to introduce... *(mumbles)* Sonic Death Monkey.

Good-natured applause. ROB steps down and beelines to LAURA. BARRY and his crew mount the stage. ROB takes a big gulp of beer.

ROB *(cont'd)* *(to LAURA)* I'm an idiot. I should have played
the record first. This place is about to get burned
down.

LAURA   It's gonna be fine. These people are ready for
anything.

          BARRY stands in front of the mic, surveying the
          crowd with a smile. He and the band all wear
          suits and ties.

BARRY   Thanks for the enthusiastic intro, Rob. We're not
called Sonic Death Monkey anymore, though,
ladies and gentlemen. We might be on the verge
of becoming the Atavistics, but we haven't decided
yet. But tonight, we are... BARRY JIVE AND THE
UPTOWN FIVE! ONE TWO THREE—

          And they launch into Marvin Gaye's 'Got To Give
          It Up,' almost flawlessly faithful to the original.
          BARRY is transformed. The crowd goes nuts, fill-
          ing the floor. ROB is stunned, begins to smile.
          LAURA takes his hand and leads him out into the
          crowd...

INT. APARTMENT. NIGHT.

          ROB is back in front of his CDs and records.

ROB   Now. A good compilation tape, like breaking up,
is hard to do and takes ages longer than it might

seem. There are a lot of rules. You gotta kick off with a killer to grab attention, then you have to take it up a notch, but not blow your wad, so maybe cool it off a notch... Anyway, I start to compile a tape in my head for Laura, full of stuff she'd like. Full of stuff that'd make her happy. For the first time, I can sort of see how it's done.

THE END